Getting into the Flow

Vincent G. Melling

Published by

Heart Space Publications
PO Box 11 90, Bakery Hill, 3350, Victoria, Australia
Tel +61 450260348
www.heartspacepublications.com
pat@heartspacebooks.com

Copyright © Vincent Gerard Melling 2022.

All rights reserved under international copyright conventions. No part of this book may be reproduced, stored in a retrieval system, or transmitted in any form or by any means electronic, mechanical, photocopying, recorded or otherwise without written permission from Heartspace Publications.

Whilst every care has been taken to check the accuracy of the information in this book, the publisher cannot be held responsible for any errors, omissions, or originality.

ISBN 978-0-6452761-6-9

Testimonial

I love this book. I have read literally hundreds of spiritual books, and even written several. This one is different. It is fresh, funny, and clever. The author's humility and intelligence shines through. Roxy, the muse, as she is called, is brilliant, witty, and demanding, exceedingly demanding, but her heart is massive. The messages, and the delivery are also fresh and profound.

If you read this book, and take the messages to heart, your life will never be the same.

Pat Grayson – CEO – Heartspace Publications

Disclaimer

This is a work of nonfiction. Some of the names and identifying details of those featured in this book have been changed to protect their privacy. Any resulting resemblance to other persons either living or dead is entirely coincidental.

This book is meant as a source of valuable information and tools for the reader. It is not meant as a substitute for direct expert assistance nor as a substitute for professional advice. If such level of assistance is required the services of a competent professional should be sought.

The publisher and the author make no representations or warranties of any kind with respect to this book or its contents. The publisher and the author do not assume any liability nor any responsibility for loss, damage or disruption caused by errors, inaccuracies, omissions, or any other inconsistencies in this book.

Dedication

"Magic is believing in yourself. If you can do that, you can make anything happen."
Johann Wolfgang von Goethe

"The world is full of magic things, patiently waiting for our senses to grow sharper."
W.B. Yeats

"And above all, watch with glittering eyes the whole world around you because the greatest secrets are always hidden in the most unlikely places. Those who don't believe in magic will never find it."
Roald Dahl

This book is dedicated to those of you who are ready to

- ... believe in and experience your greatness,
- ... sharpen your senses,
- ... watch your world with eagle eyes,
- ... and find the magic that's already there in you and in your life.

Contents

Testimonial i
Disclaimer ii
Dedication iii
Preface Living in Magic and Flow vi
Introducing Roxy.. vii
Part 1 What does "the flow" really look like? The story of how this book came to be written. 1
    Chapter 1 In which I complain about how the universe seems to favor everybody else 3
    Chapter 2 From January in Brisbane to December at Uluru 5
    Chapter 3 The evening of the solstice. 23
    Chapter 4 After Uluru 29
Part 2 What getting in the flow can do for you – and what you can do for the flow...35
    Chapter 5 Why would you want to get into the flow?..............37
    Chapter 6 What do you really want? 51
    Chapter 7 The seductive power of your comfort zone 65
    Chapter 8 Why should the universe help us, anyway?............77
Part 3 Understanding the flow 89
    Chapter 9 Alignment..91
    Chapter 10 What is structure and why is it so important?.....111
    Chapter 11 What is energy and why is it important? 127
Part 4 Intuitive skills and tools for getting into the flow 141
    Chapter 12 Introduction to the skills and tools 143
    Chapter 13 Meet your intuition with the Innosence exercise 147
    Chapter 14 Symbols..157
    Chapter 15 Circles...169
    Chapter 16 Your shadow...179

Part 5 Putting the tools to work 201
    Chapter 17 Alignment 203
    Chapter 18 Creating Choices 215
    Chapter 19 Creative Tension 235
    Chapter 20 Energy 251

Part 6 Living in Flow 271
    Chapter 21 Engaging the flow 273

Part 7 Conclusion and summary 290

Epilogue 297
    Over to you 298
    Continuing your journey into intuition 299
    A final, super-synchronistic word from the Hopi elders 301

Appendices 303
    Appendix 1 Exercises and resources 305
    Appendix 2 Vincent's experience with the innosense meditation 319
    Appendix 3 Quiz answers 321

About the author(s) 325
    Vincent by Vincent 326
    Roxy by Vincent 327
    Roxy by Roxy 329
    Vincent by Roxy 331
    Acknowledgements 332
    Glossary 335
    Work further with Vincent 338
    Reach out to Vincent 340

Preface
Living in Magic and Flow

In early 2020, I first heard about the global meditation planned for the 2020 December solstice at Uluru (also known as Ayers Rock) in the center of Australia, and the background stories from aboriginal sources. At first I felt curious, then intrigued, then finally compelled to make the trip to Uluru for this event – even though the invitation was to simply join the meditation from anywhere in the world.

My journey to Uluru, my experiences there, what came before and what happened since all served to teach me this powerful lesson

> **Key insight:**
> That there is a universal energetic flow, and when we align with it through finding our true nature, our true path, we begin to live in magic and flow, creating what we consider impossible with a fraction of the physical effort, mental stress, and spiritual angst. The most common ways that this magic shows up are coincidences, synchronicities, perfect timing[1], unlooked-for opportunities, and out of the blue (re-)connections.

This book tells of how this lesson came to me through the events of 2020. It gives the foundational principles that underpin magic and flow; and of the intuitive skills and tools that I had learned and practiced over several years. This has enabled me to recognize and understand the lessons from those events. I share this with you so that you too can learn to live in magic and flow.

---

1 Some in the New Age community use the term 'divine timing'; for example, they might say 'your soulmate will arrive in divine timing'. It's as if a higher power is deciding what happens; and the when is arbitrary and random. I prefer 'perfect timing' which, for me, implies alignment with my purpose and true potential, and a co-creation between higher powers and me, where the magic fits in beautifully with action I have taken. It has the feel of a piece of a jigsaw dropping into place and enhancing or completing the full picture.

Introducing Roxy

Roxy says she needs no introduction. She's probably right. She usually is. Usually? She says always. So, instead of a conventional introduction, here's how I met her.

Met her?

She ambushed me.

I'm a member of a writer's group who share an intuitive approach to writing. We meet weekly for working sessions. And, about a month into writing the book, in one of those sessions we had a simple exercise. We each had to connect with our muse and then write some more of our respective books. That's exactly what everybody else in the group did.

Not me. When I connected to my intuition, I didn't get the sweet, helpful, obliging muse I'd been working with up to that point. No. Just the opposite. For no reason at all – or, at least that I could discern – I started writing in verse from a deep, deep inner place. The climax read :-

> I'm no demure old-fashioned muse
> With careful phrases, pleasant to use
> I'm a brazen showgirl right up front...

At which point, as I was wondering what outrageous rhyme would come through next, thankfully, the facilitator called time. At the start of the group meeting I had no idea that I even needed another muse. But what did I know?

Just as the universe had made me an offer I couldn't refuse (to write this book), now it brought me Roxy. She's made writing the book fun, brought it to life, and held my nose to the proverbial grindstone while leading me through some breathtaking insights. It has been another of the many pieces of magic on the path to creating this book.

What I get from Roxy are ideas, words, and little packets of knowing or energy that I have to unpack. Over the course of the book, her voice has evolved to come through in a no-nonsense pan-loaf (posh) Edinburgh accent. When I listen, I hear a female version of Sean Connery. The rest is history, as the saying goes. Because history is, was and always will be there to be created.

Welcome Roxy!

Part 1

What does "the flow" really look like?
The story of how this book came to be written.

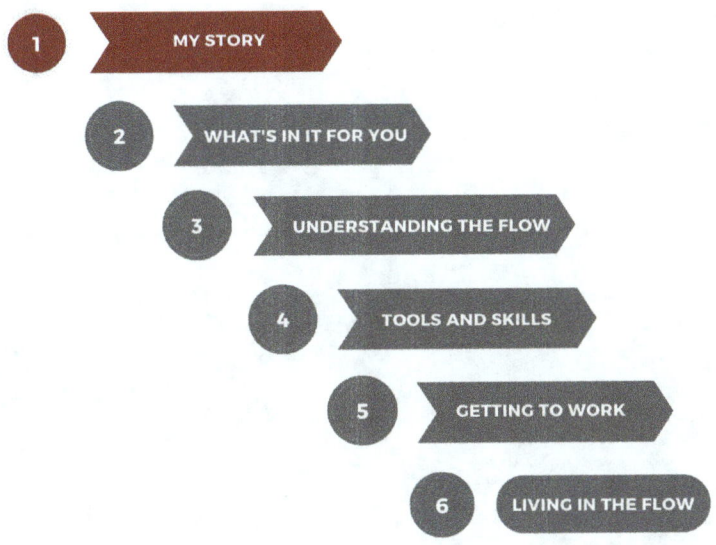

Chapter 1

In which I complain about how the universe seems to favor everybody else ...

Now what follows here, I swear, is totally true.
I'm just that kind of person, wouldn't lie to you.
See, the story below cries out to be told.
And I know you will see, as the steps unfold,
**That the universe will help us when
we're in the flow.
We've just got to open up, align and let go.**

It used to make me volcanic-mad.
When I'd set intentions, nothing happened. So sad.
For everyone else, it worked, never a doubt;
But nothing I asked for ever seemed to work out.

Geoff's a yoga teacher mate, and he'd just set
an intention for the students that he's going to get.
It feels that all he has to do, I swear, is just ask.
And that exact number turns up in his class.

Adriana, Adriana, knows how to set intentions.
Calls people to her workshops 'cross many dimensions.
From Intuition sees their names. So magical.
Before they even sign up.
Now ain't that fantastical?

And even my some time-housemate Pammy.
When we used to go shopping, she'd get so jammy.
Manifest parking spots right next to the door.
I swear I couldn't take it anymore

You see I'd
    set intentions and get sweet FA
Didn't know why. Didn't know what to say.
    I used to ask the universe WTF
do I have to do to get results like Geoff?

The universe stayed silent,
    Biding its time,
Waiting, like forever, for the planets to align.

Then ...
    eleven months before that stellar conjunction[1]
the universe spoke, through an unwelcome malfunction
in the bushwalking plan that I'd made for the day
with my longtime friend Kate. She stood me up.
Not OK.

---

1 Roxy says
Yes, there are going to be some pedant peasants (not that I'm ever judgmental) who read this and will point out that the conjunction in question was, in fact, planetary not stellar. Technically, you're correct. I hope that makes you feel better. However, you do need to learn about poetic license. Fortunately, there's a six-week training for people like you that Vincent plan to runs called "Learn Yourself Poetic License" for only $25,000. It will be the best value of your life. You need this. Pre-register here...(https://vincentgmelling.com/lypl-home)

Chapter 2

From January in Brisbane to December at Uluru

Vincent

Roxy, can you explain to me why TF did I ever come to write this book in the first place?

Roxy

Really? You are asking me? Haven't you any idea? It is your book.

Vincent

I know I had to write it because the universe told me to. It's like a mission from God. But I don't really get why.

I had a bucket list trip to Uluru[2] after the COVID lockdowns ended in 2020. It was an amazing experience. Fantastic. Memorable. Why couldn't it all have ended right there?

Why was it that, of all the days that I'd lived in my sixty-something years, of all the experiences in my life, these few days were the ones that the universe – through my intuition – started jumping up and down and screaming at me, DEMANDING that I write this book about them?

Roxy

Vincent, have you ever considered why it took you sixty-

---

2   Vincent says
Uluru is also known – and is probably best known outside Australia – as Ayers Rock. Uluru is the First Nation's Peoples name for the Sacred Rock. So we use that out of respect.

something years to create an experience that would serve as a starting point for that special book you were always going to write? That special book that always seemed to show up when you did a visioning exercise on your life? That special book that your intuitive friends always told you that you had inside?

> **Key insight:**
> We all have a purpose and true (or greatest) potential in life and it will find ways to come back to us over and over until we take action on it.

Have you ever considered why it took you over thirty years from the day you first touched down in Australia to finally arriving at Uluru?

Vincent

Now you're just making me feel bad.

Roxy

Bad. Now that's a loaded word. It can mean evil and cruel. Is that how you feel?

Vincent

No. Not bad like that.

Roxy

Or perhaps you mean guilty, and a touch ashamed?

Vincent

Well, yes. It's uncomfortable.

Roxy

Good. Making you feel uncomfortable? That's my job.

I'll do whatever it takes to get you to create this book.

> **Key insight:**
> Even when we know what action we have to take, that action that is aligned with our purpose and true potential in life, we often experience resistance, a reluctance to take that action. This will be revisited later in the book.

Vincent

You're not answering my original question.
Why me? Why this book? Why now (or then)?
Why did the universe choose this time in my life to write the book?

Roxy

You know the answer.

Vincent

No I don't. Otherwise I wouldn't be asking my all-seeing all-knowing muse.

Yes, that's you.

Roxy

Oh, but you do know the answer.

You're just playing dumb. That seems to be common enough with you humans. You refuse to see the obvious, not because it's not visible but because it's not comfortable.

So, let me ask you the questions. What was special about that trip to Uluru?

Vincent

Well, it was the first opportunity we had to get out of Melbourne after the COVID lockdowns.

Roxy

Maybe. But it's the wrong answer and you know it. Will you

stop playing stupid, stop spouting nonsense and stop trying to steer the conversation away from anything remotely uncomfortable for you?

You could have gone anywhere in Australia when that lockdown ended. You could have gone to Surfers Paradise or Byron Bay or even the Barrier Reef.

What was so special that you made a trip to Uluru?

Does that sound like just any random "freedom-from-COVID" trip?

Vincent

Well, it was that video that Donald got me to watch. I guess I was curious.

Roxy

Indeed. Wasn't it the universe that put you on the path in the first place? And helped you every step of the way?

Vincent

What do you mean?

Roxy

Well tell me, what brought you to Brisbane in January 2020?

Vincent

I do a practice called shaking[3]. Every year, our shaking community gathers for a five-day retreat in northern New South Wales. It ended on a Sunday and I planned to head to Brisbane on the Monday so I could join the shakers' group there on the Tuesday evening. Kate was one of the shakers; we

---

3 Roxy says

Bio-energy meditation, also known as shaking, is a meditative yogic practice. It was created in its current form by Ratu Bagus, a Bali-based guru. He passed into the astral in August 2021 but his work, his ashram, his astral presence and the love and energy he brought live on. Vincent spends an inordinate amount of time on this practice, although I have to admit it does keep him pretty healthy in mind body and spirit, which he needs because we have a lot of books to write together.

have a soul connection; and, during the retreat, we'd arranged the bushwalk.

Roxy

Very good, VG[4]. So it wasn't just the normal version of you that ended up in Brisbane. It was the version of you, sensitized and energized from the retreat that turned up. Let's remember that.

You had a lovely bushwalking date lined up. You have a great friend with the deep connection and with whom you could have profound conversations. You had the most beautiful day for it, and then it was all whisked away from you. Just like that. Did you have any sort of warning?

Vincent

No. No warning at all. It took a series of unanswered phone calls and text messages for the reality to sink in. It finally dawned on me that there would be no bushwalk.

Roxy

That was pretty dramatic, wasn't it?

Vincent

Dramatic? More of an anticlimax.

Roxy

So how did you feel? How did you react?

Vincent

I was so disappointed. I felt really let down, abandoned, and confused.

Roxy

Vincent, let me remind you, this is a book, not therapy. That's

---

4 Vincent says
There's bound to be somebody that asks why Roxy says this. The answer is simply that VG are my initials.

enough of the pity party. Tell me, how did you react? What did you do?

Vincent

You did ask me how I felt...

Fortunately, I was able to get back to a positive frame of mind and set to work on creating a Plan B for the day.

Roxy

And plan B involved you calling your friend Donald who insisted you watch the video that put the idea of the trip into your head in the first place. He insisted it would change how you see everything.

Was that a coincidence? A Coincidence with a capital C?

Remember, you'd just come from a retreat. You were sensitized, energized and receptive to what might land in your highest good. And that's the message you received.

Vincent

You're saying the universe set me up to miss out on that bushwalk so that I'd find out about the prophecies?

Roxy

Isn't that obvious? Oh my goodness, how we spirits have to spell it out, step by step by step to you humans. Sometimes, I think it is indeed fortunate we have an eternity – even if you don't.

Yes, it got you into the flow.

So didn't you want to watch that video?

Vincent

No. I was time-poor. I'm always time-poor. I actually didn't want to spend an hour watching that video.

Roxy

But obviously you did, eventually. What led you to watching the video when you had so many excuses and so little time?

Vincent

It took me about a month to get to it. It didn't seem important.

Roxy

Well, clearly it wasn't urgent. But it must have been important. Otherwise it would never have made it above, let's say, number four hundred and twenty-three on your humungously long to-do list.

Vincent

I'm not attached to that to-do-list. I have tons of things on there that aren't important and I probably won't get to. It's just so I don't lose track of what really is important.

Roxy

And so we deduce that watching that video must have been really important for you. Why do you think that was?

Vincent

I don't know.

Roxy

Oh, but you do know. It's something else that's uncomfortable, that you just don't want to talk about it. But you're going to have to talk about it anyway. Why do you think that watching that video was so important to you when you had no idea about what the content was?

Vincent

It must have been Donald's insistence and the sense of urgency in his voice over the phone. Usually he's pretty laid back, amusing and gets a lot done in a very matter-of-fact way. I must have felt a different energy about him that day.

Roxy

So you received a message from Donald in that call, in a way you could delay but never say no to taking action. Do you understand that the reason you resonated so strongly with that call was that the message in it was always on your soul's agenda? Do you realize that it was your intuition crying out to you to stop making excuses and start watching the video?

You've probably never even entertained that idea.

Tell me, does that sound true to you?

Vincent

What? That my intuition was crying out to me to stop making excuses?

It's not a surprise. It's always doing that.

Roxy

Vincent! You are right about the excuses ... But again you're refusing to answer the question because what's obvious is rather uncomfortable for you.

(forcefully)

Now tell me, does it sound true to you that you received this insistent message from Donald in a way that would ensure that you watched the video?

Vincent

S'pose so.

Roxy

I'll consider that to be a 'Yes'. Finally! Thank goodness for that. We can move on.

Now please tell me about your reaction to the video.

Vincent

Well, actually the information in it was pretty mind-blowing. The December solstice in 2020 would see a shift in global consciousness. The turning on of a key energy system in the Earth, akin to ley lines. A return to the Earth of the Pleiadians[5]. All long-foretold in ancient prophecies of First Nations peoples across Australia. They called it the start of "the change".

Roxy

Well, you wouldn't have come across that in the news or on TV, would you? It sounds to me that getting this message was the next step in the flow. You watched the video and the story really engaged you.

And so, now I expect you're trying to tell me you thought 'that was pretty neat' and then did nothing?

Vincent

Well, yes. I didn't have the money and I didn't have the time and I promptly forgot all about it.

Roxy

Promptly forgot all about it?

How could you forget about something as important, as profound, as potentially pivotal in the history of humanity as that?

Vincent

I just did and carried on with my life. I had to keep working.

---

5 The Pleiadians are the inhabitants of the Pleiades star system.

There are multiple belief systems held by New Age and First Nations people that makes it difficult to be clear about them.

Most commonly-held beliefs characterize them as being physically and genetically like us inhabitants of Earth. They are more spiritually advanced and are actively helping us into a more spiritually aligned, earth friendly way of life.

Roxy

That didn't last long, did it?

Vincent

That's because COVID came, and we got locked down, and I couldn't work.

Roxy

So I suppose you just put your feet up and started stressing about what you'd do for money. Am I right or am I right?

Vincent

Pretty much. I had access to a government scheme to keep me going financially. And, in that time, my online communities got created. The shaking community and the Natural Success intuition trainings kept me busy; and I took up jogging and started to get fit.

Roxy

So what changed? In amongst all the busy-ness of your lockdown life, what brought the story in the video back into your awareness?

Vincent

Some COVID support money finally came through, and all of a sudden I had funds. And the COVID numbers began to come down and I could see the eventual end of the lockdowns was on its way.

Roxy

And was that just lucky? Or was it in the flow?

What was the first thing you thought about when you had the money?

Vincent

The Thai takeaway I'd been promising myself all lockdown?

Roxy

Nonsense. Perhaps I shouldn't have asked. It's lucky I don't need you to tell me. I know. You magically remembered about that video and how much you really wanted to make the trip, didn't you? That was your soul calling, wasn't it?

It was the very first thing that came to you — even before that Thai food. If it was more important than that, then the video must have been exceptionally important.

Vincent

The Thai food was a close second.

Roxy

Humans!

Stop trying to side track me. Again.

The idea of a trip had always been calling, except that you hadn't been listening. You'd have to admit that wouldn't you?

Vincent

I guess so.

Roxy

So what crossed your mind when you finally responded? What action came to you?

Vincent

I thought about it a bit and decided to do a road trip. I love road trips for the peace and quiet and open space they give me. It would take three days. I'd always wanted to see Coober Pedy, the mostly-underground opal mining town at the end of day two. And my friend Aurora lived in Maitland, South Australia, a little way past Adelaide, not far off my route north and a perfect spot to end day one. She was always bugging me to come over so I got in touch. It turned out she wanted to join me on the trip. With some of her family.

Roxy

How did that make you feel?

Vincent

It added a party feel to the trip. It felt really good. Suddenly I found myself looking forward to it.

Roxy

So having provided the call and the funding, the universe now gave you the promise of company, of fun and locked you in to doing the trip, didn't it?

Vincent

Locked me in?

Roxy

After that you didn't even consider not going, did you?

Vincent

I did have one fear. The only thing that now stood in the way of going was COVID. The case numbers were falling but at this point (late September 2020), we were still locked down in Melbourne.

Roxy

So what happened?

Vincent

The case numbers kept falling. Restrictions were eased and eased again. By early November, we were pretty freed up; but Melbourne was still designated a hot spot by the other Australian states, so we couldn't leave Victoria.

Roxy

And then?

Vincent

Finally, in late November, Victoria made it to green status. We were no longer a hotspot, and we were able to travel.

Roxy

So the trip was on?

Vincent

Yes and no. There was a COVID flare-up in South Australia and that was now a hot spot.

Roxy

So close and yet so far. So the trip was off, then?

Vincent

Not exactly. I decided to get out of Victoria before there was another flare up here – they were springing up out of the blue everywhere. So I booked a flight to Alice Springs. And on December 6th two weeks before the solstice, I landed there, made it through the Northern Territory border control and heaved a huge sense of relief.

Roxy

So the trip really was on after all? What about all those coincidences and all that perfect timing that needed to be in place so that you could get up there? Somehow, the universe found a way to get you into the Northern Territory, didn't it?

Vincent

I suppose so.

Roxy

So you made it into the Northern Territory, had some down time in Alice Springs, rented a car, and drove the four and a half hours through the red center of Australia to the Yulara resort, close to Uluru. What had happened to Aurora and her family? Were they locked down?

Getting into the Flow

Vincent

Actually no, they weren't. In the end, just Aurora and her father, Mark, drove up from Maitland. They made their way to Alice Springs and we met there the evening before I left for Yulara. They headed down there a different way, via Kings' Canyon and arrived in Yulara a day later.

Roxy

So you were abandoned again? At least for a night? Another evening of poor little old me?

Vincent

It actually worked out perfectly.

Roxy

Really? So the Universe had something lined up for you? I'm shocked. Tell me more.

Vincent

I had another friend, Tess, who had already arrived. I called her, we met, and she invited me to join her and her friends at Uluru at sunrise the following day. We had a wonderful morning. We were able to walk all the way round and get a feel for the size and all the different energies around it. We spent over three hours as we stopped and met people on the way, including a ranger. It was 11:30am when we left, the sun was high and it had got pretty hot.

Roxy

Well, that's not surprising. Weren't you in the middle of desert country? Weren't you expecting 35 degrees [*just under 100° Fahrenheit*] every day?

Vincent

I was. That would not be good when you're camping. But it wasn't like that. They had a particularly cool and wet summer in the Northern Territory that year. More like 26 degrees [*78° Fahrenheit*]. Very pleasant.

Roxy

It does make it feel like the universe was looking after you, doesn't it? What happened when Aurora and Mark arrived?

Vincent

They arrived later that day. When they'd set up their tents, we decided to go back to Uluru and drive round. Just as well because I was shattered from walking. It was a beautiful afternoon. Then we agreed to head to Kata Tjuta for sunrise the following morning.

Roxy

And were you able to get up?

Vincent

Of course.

You don't believe me? Seriously? The date and timestamps are on my photos.

Aurora and Mark were a little later than planned but we were on the road by seven. When we got there, it was surprisingly cool. They wanted to do quite a challenging walk so I said I'd go halfway; but I ended up doing it all – and finding it easy.

The funny thing was, on the way back out of the National Park, a little after 10am, there was traffic in the opposite lane behaving strangely. I recall one SUV coming from the opposite direction trying to do a U-turn through the median strip just before the park entrance.

When we got back, we learned they'd closed the National Park. The campsite grapevine said that it was because there was another COVID outbreak – this one in Sydney where at least two flights had come from. The local Aboriginal people wanted to play it safe so they closed the park. And others on the grapevine said it was to keep everyone else away from disturbing the secret solstice ceremonies. Who knows the truth? Do you, Roxy?

Roxy

Of course – but it's not for you to know and it doesn't matter.

So you got to spend a day and a half in the National Park before they shut it?

Vincent

Yes.

Roxy

And you actually got to Uluru in the first place, even though another one of your friends got turned back from her flight from Sydney. This was because of a COVID outbreak was close to where she lived and they would not let her fly?

Vincent

Well, yes. Obviously.

Roxy

You always wanted to visit Uluru and you get there despite COVID and you spend a day and a half in the National Park; and then they shut it just as you had finished deeply connecting with it, and as you were driving out.

Have you ever considered just how much you were in the flow? Just how much the universe was helping you? This sounds like a bucket list trip that goes better than perfect.

How much better can it get?

> **Key insight:**
> Magic and flow show up as coincidences, synchronicities, perfect timing, unlooked-for opportunities, and phone calls out of the blue. That's not a complete list – these are the commonest.

What happened next?

Vincent

Here's what I wrote about the evening of the solstice (after the maps).

Maps of my trip

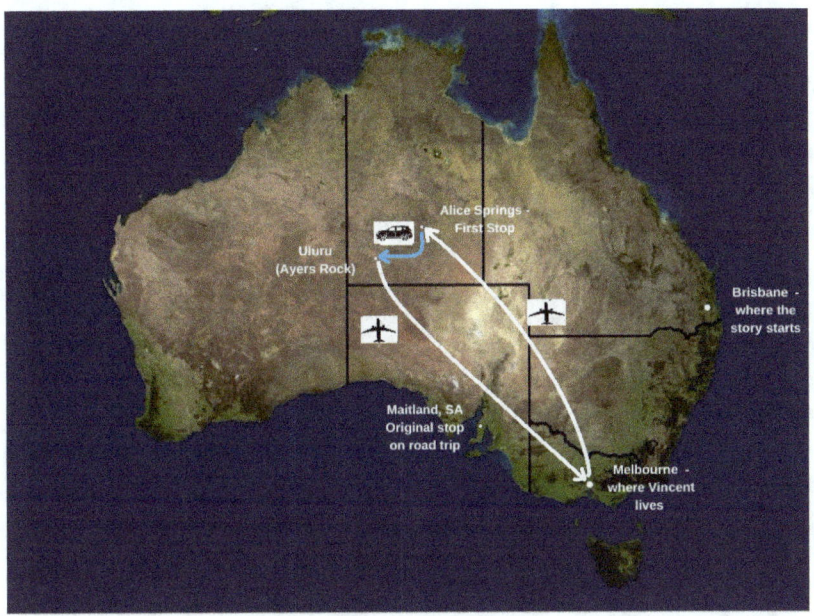

Figure 1: Derivative work: Harpagon (talk) based on image created by NASA. Australia Satellite Map / Location Map
Image: Australia_location_map.png: Diceman
https://commons.wikimedia.org/wiki/File:Australia_satellite_states.jpg

*Additional Car and aircraft icons created using assets from Freepik.com
Additional markup by Vincent G. Melling*

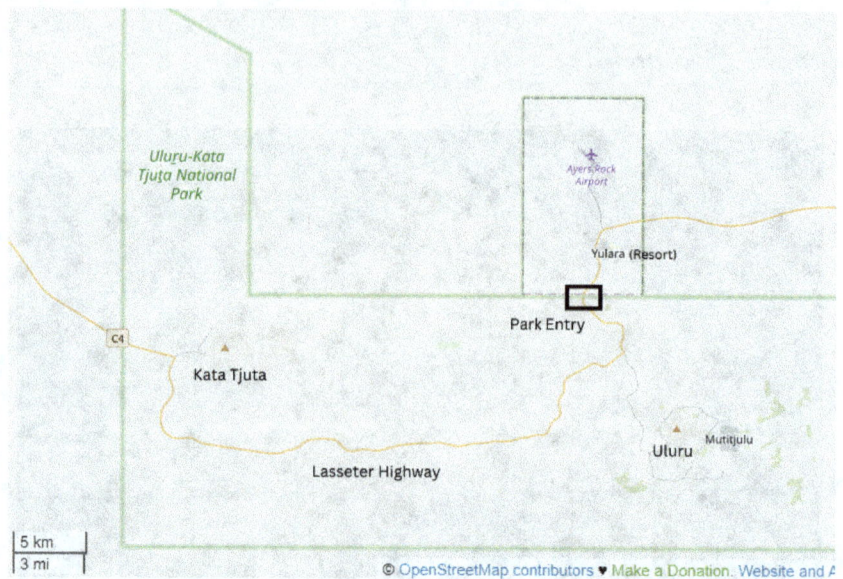

*Figure 2 Map © OpenStreetMap Map of Uluru Kata Tjuta National Park contributors (https://www.openstreetmap.org/copyright).
The data is available under the Open Database License
Additional markup by Vincent G Melling*

Chapter 3

The evening of the solstice.

Beside our campsite stood a little hill
Dusty and sandy. Nondescript. But still
It offered us a wide expansive view
Of heavens and plains and out to Uluru

Figure 3: Vincent G. Melling Uluru from the hill adjacent to the Yulara campsite. 22 December 2020

The solstice, long-awaited, now came fast
The evening we had come here for. At last
Forty-strong, we climbed the hill and saw
A skyscape like I'd never seen before
Across the vastness of the sky unfold-
ed clouds of pink and red and burnished gold
Illuminated by the setting sun
And we were awestruck... every single one

And in the distance, somber Uluru
Awaiting the night's events. An era new

And in the clouds, a gap, unearthly blue
'Pleiadians' said the elders, We all knew they knew,

Figure 4: Vincent G. Melling Sky to the west of Yulara from the hill adjacent to the Yulara campsite. 22 December 2020

Figure 5: Vincent G. Melling Solstice sunset on the hill adjacent to the Yulara campsite. 22 December 2020

Half seven came. We sat in meditation
With thousands 'cross the world. Synchronization
Sending love and energy unto
Mother Earth through sacred Uluru

Figure 6: Vincent G. Melling Uluru and skyscape from the hill adjacent to the Yulara campsite. 22 December 2020

And finally, confirmation through a sign
Those wilful, crazy planets had aligned
Saturn and Jupiter high in the darkened sky
Herald the new era for humanity.

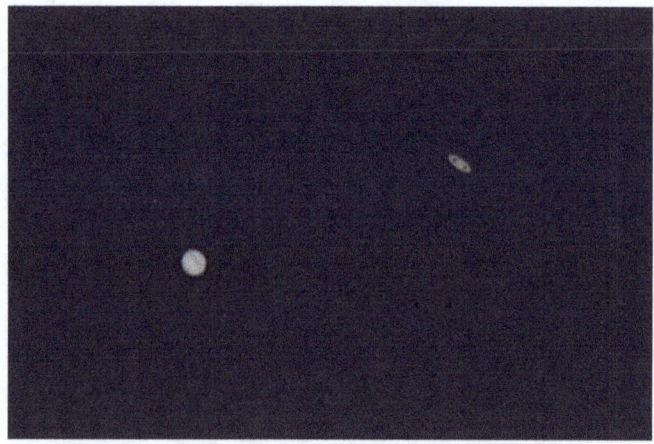

Figure 7: Steve Fung Great Conjunction of Jupiter and Saturn, 17:50 CST, 21 December 2020. This file is licensed under the Creative Commons Attribution-Share Alike 2.0 Generic license.

Chapter 4

After Uluru

Roxy

    Well, Vincent, I loved the words and loved the photos. I've worked with Pleiadians in the distant past. They're such a lovely race, and so much less trouble than you humans, but somehow they're a little too perfect to be really interesting. They got me to use my famous literary skills to help create the maintenance manual for the interstellar hyper-drive they use in their ships. A maintenance manual! Such a waste of my boundless literary talent.

Vincent

    Now you're kidding me. You could tell me – and all of humanity – how to build an interstellar hyper-drive? Seriously?

Roxy

    Not exactly. I'm sorry I can't. I can only tell you how to clean it inside, top up the lubricants and coolant, replace the space-dust filters, clean the contacts – and there are so many contacts and they need to be kept pristine. It's much like a car service, really. I'm sorry to disappoint you.

    (pauses)

    So, tell me, what happened after that evening. Did everything stop flowing?

    Did you say 'Thank you Universe. Been there, done that. Job done?'

Vincent

    Well, here's the funny thing, Roxy. No.

The coincidences kept coming. Why I was still in Yulara in the days after the solstice, by chance I met a friend who lived only a short walk away from me in Melbourne. I hadn't seen him for a while and we had a great catch-up chat. What was interesting is that we'd always met in groups and never spoken one-on-one. And it was timely because he was planning to move out of Victoria.

Another friend who had also come to Yulara invited me to do some healing work and paid me for it. I wasn't expecting that.

While I was in the campsite's food prep shelter one lunchtime, I met Robert Jameson, author of *The Bali to Bairnsdale Alignment*. He has a deep knowledge of ley lines including the ones that pass through Uluru; and I enjoyed a long and fascinating conversation with him.

Over the following two days, I met other friends I hadn't seen for years – including two in the café at the Ayers Rock Airport as I was waiting to board my flight back to Melbourne.

Roxy

So, you were in the flow afterwards? Very good, VG.

So tell me, because I am curious, did everything stop flowing once you landed back in Melbourne?

Vincent

Well, here's the even funnier thing. No, it didn't.

I arrived back on December 23rd and I had to rush to get some work completed and finalize my Christmas shopping. Then I spent the next few days with family and friends, and so it was in the quieter days, early in the new year, that my intuition spoke.

It said to me;
'you know you've got to write this into a book, now, don't you?'

Roxy

So, tell me, how did that make you feel?

Vincent

My heart sank.

I'd done three major writing projects before. They had all been a ton of work and gone nowhere. Complete failures. I didn't feel up to another one. I didn't feel I had the energy.

Roxy

But we're here talking now, so something must have changed. What was it?

Vincent

Actually, nothing changed.

Although my heart sank, I had a deep, deep knowing that this had to be done because it was just true for me to do it. I knew from my work that sometimes it's true to create something you have resistance to and you just have to be with the discomfort that's there in that resistance.

> **Key insight:**
> This is a recap that we all experience resistance, a topic that revisited later in the book.

So I got out the writing course which I'd bought six months previously but not looked at since; and I started studying it.

Roxy

Oh, so you were expecting to write a book at some point then? It was pretty convenient that you had pre-selected and purchased your writing course already, wasn't it? In the flow, wouldn't you say?

Vincent

I guess I must have been. Come to think of it, when I bought the course, it was about the third time that I'd had the opportunity to take it one way or another. That was some months before the idea of the Uluru trip had even resurfaced in my awareness.

Intuition had shown me back in 2014 that I would write a book. But it had never shown me what it was about.

> **Key insight:**
> Our intuition calls us back to our true path repeatedly, in different ways, until we take action. Meanwhile it may offer us opportunities to pick up the skills and develop the talents we'll need.

Roxy

So how else did the universe support you to write this book?

Vincent

My friends Leah and Jamie mentioned separately that they were in a writers group. I asked about it; and, the next thing I knew, I was in.

Roxy

And did the universe support you in any other way?

Vincent

Not that I can think of.

Roxy

Well try engaging your brain then. There must be one last thing.

Vincent

It's all about you isn't it?

Roxy

All about me?

I'm a muse and a powerful spirit guide and you insinuate that I'm somehow egocentric? How dare you!

Vincent

But it is. It was you. That you turned up in the early days. I wrote about it in the Introduction.

Roxy

Ah, yes. Thank you. I came as soon as I got the call from the universe, once you were in the flow with the book. Of course the last – or should I say the next way – you received support from the universe was getting to work with me. And, let's be honest, tell me Vincent, where would this book be without me to inspire you and poke and prod you and get you digging deep?

(pause)

And working?

(pause)

The universe has continued to help us along in so many ways since then with this book; but that's for elsewhere. We've reached the natural end of story of how this book came to be.

Now we have work to do.

Our readers want to know what you do to engage and create all this magic and flow in your life; and how they can do it too.

And it's time for you... sorry, for us to tell them.

> **Key insight:**
> The universe helped create this book with magic and flow in many ways. The rest of the book will help you understand how to engage that energy and create magic for yourselves in your lives.

Part 2

What getting in the flow can do for you – and what you can do for the flow

Chapter 5

Why would you want to get into the flow?

How can we get the flow like in Vincent's story?

Roxy

Anybody who has read your story will say that it's amazing.

Anyone?
Well, there will always to be somebody who will say 'it's complete nonsense, all rainbows, sunshine and unicorns, just make-believe'. However, we're not writing this for them, they won't have read this far anyway, and they're certainly welcome to slave away at jobs they barely tolerate for the rest of their lives and miss out on the magic and flow that is available to them.

If that's you, please stop reading now.

So any of you readers who get this far will say that's an amazing story.

Welcome to all of you reading this. You're our Flow Posse.

But
And you'll always come up with all these buts[1],

---

1 Roxy says

When you humans say the word 'but', it's a sure sign that everything that preceded the word 'but' can safely be ignored; for example, I'm not a racist but... It is also like a flashing warning sign to watch out for, as an excuse is probably coming up. The more emphatic the 'but', the bigger, the badder and the more outrageous the excuse will be. That's why I call you humans but-heads.

Because you humans have been conditioned by your so-called society to be but-heads, so there's always a but …

What you're probably asking is
'how can I get into the flow like that?'

Now although this book is a serious metaphysical text, which comes to you humans with love, tough love, you will still try to make it all about you.
You are so self-centered, so needy, so deeply mired in lack-energy.
Humans!

(exaggerated sigh)

Not that I'm ever, ever judgmental.

The question you humans should be asking

So I'm going to answer the question you should be asking; which is;
'What is getting into the flow all about? And why would I want it?'

And this is going to sound really simple.
Why wouldn't you want it?

It's simply how you humans were created to be.
Take a breath and let that sink in.
It's something that's always been available to you.
But I can sense you may have a wee bit of trouble understanding and – particularly – accepting that.

Key insight:
The top question arising from Vincent's story is
'What is getting into the flow all about? And why would I want it?'
The answer is simply, Why wouldn't you want it?
It's how humans were created to be.

What's the wrong meaning of going with the flow?

Vincent

Well, I'd say that most of us humans haven't experienced the flow and so we don't believe in it or know it exists. Or even worse, we make up stories about what flow is, usually as an excuse for our stuff ups or for being lazy. You know, like I don't want to clean the bathroom, just going with the flow.

Roxy

Thank goodness I'm a spirit being and so have no need to use your bathroom.

Vincent

People just say that.
I do keep my bathroom clean.
And I certainly don't call not cleaning "going with the flow".

Roxy

What do you call it then? And don't try and pretend your place is always spotless.

Vincent

That's not the point, Roxy. I don't call it going with the flow because it isn't.

> **Key insight:**
> Getting into the flow is not about taking the easy way out in daily life.

What's it like when you don't live in the flow?

Roxy

OK, Vincent. I believe you. You said that most of you humans haven't experienced the flow and so you don't believe or know it exists. What does that mean for you? What does that lead to? Have you had any experiences from the time before you knew about the flow?

Vincent

Well...

Roxy

Sorry, I even ask silly questions from time to time. Of course you've had experiences from when you're not in the flow. Tell me about them.

Vincent

Well, you have to work hard to get anything done successfully. Get anything done successfully? Get everything done successfully.
Life feels hard, difficult, challenging. It feels like it lacks meaning, and that you're not getting anywhere for all the work.

Roxy

You? Work hard? Do you have any conception of what that might mean?

Vincent

And you have to put a lot of emotion and energy in to make things happen.

Roxy

And what else?

Vincent

You end up learning to deal with failure.

Roxy

And I'm guessing you've experienced plenty of that and very uncomfortable it must have been too. But I will not allow you to suck me in to a pity party. No.

> **Key insight:**
> Life outside the flow feels hard, difficult, challenging, lacking meaning and it feels like a lot of work with nothing to show for it.

What is living in the flow like?

I have another question instead. Compared to being out of it, what's living in the flow like?

Vincent

Life feels light and easy. Sometimes there's less work – much less – and sometimes there's just as much work but it flows and feels easy.

And there's always a sense that you are being held by a bigger power and carried on your journey to successfully create the end results you seek.

Roxy

Exactly. Beautiful.

What exactly is being in the flow?

Vincent

But if leaving the bathroom cleaning is not being in the flow what exactly is being in the flow?

Roxy

You know, you've felt it.

Vincent

But how would you explain it to the people who haven't?

And why are you rolling your eyes?

Roxy

Vincent. I'm a powerful cosmic multidimensional mega-being. So you must realize that what you're asking me is like me asking you to explain algebra to a dog. Oh yes, the dog will smile and wag her tail if you ask her if she wants to learn algebra in that "walkies" tone of voice. It doesn't mean she has a clue what you're talking about. She just thinks she's going on a walk. I bet our dog-owning readers are trying this out now for themselves ...

So. The flow for humans...

The simple version.
The really simple version.
The version so simple that even Sun[2] readers will understand...

... is

...that there is a frequency of energy that flows in the universe and through the universe. It's a frequency that combines the energy of life, love and consciousness; of expansion, evolution and creation.

And any conscious being can tune in to that frequency and harness that energy to create what they want in life. Even your cats and dogs do – how else do you think they manifest food, shelter, and love for a lifetime? Do they have to work hard for their living? Imagine trying to tell that to a cat.

> **Key insight:**
> To get into the flow, you have to tune in to the energy of life, love and consciousness; of expansion, evolution and creation that flows in the universe and harness that energy to create what they want in life.

---

2 Vincent says
The Sun is a UK newspaper for people who just like to look at the pictures.

What won't the flow help with?

However, there is a catch. That frequency, that flow cannot be used to create just anything. You know, like that perennial desire all you humans seem to have to win the lottery. You can't use it for that. That's not the flow.

By the way did you win anything last week?

Vincent

If I had I wouldn't tell you. That's the first rule of winning the lottery.

Roxy

I'll take that as a no.

Vincent

That's not what I said.

Roxy

I know that's not what you said and I'm still taking it as a no.

I thought not. And haven't you ever wondered why? Ever?

(sigh)

Of course you have. But you still have that part of you driven by a lack mentality, that seems to pop up on cue every week when you're at the shops. And winning the lottery is so, so seductive. And so you always end up getting a ticket, don't you.

(sigh)

You need to align

Anyway, the catch is that if you want help from the universe, the very first thing you have to do is align with it. Do you understand that?

Vincent

Yes.

Roxy

Well, I'll take your word for it. You've done a lot of work on it. But most humans? Do you give two hoots about aligning with the universe? Most of you expect the universe to do their bidding... like a servant.

And if they do spare a thought to alignment, what stories do they make up about how that looks?

(sighs again)

Do you think the universe has ever written a book on what its agenda is so you can align with it? Created a set of tablets? Drawn a diagram in nature with crop circles or rivers and lakes and mountains? That all sounds far too complicated.

> **Key insight:**
> Getting into the flow won't help with everything in life. It will help most in those parts of your life that are aligned with your true nature and purpose.

And what do we get when we're in the flow?

Vincent

I guess not.

So how do we align?

Roxy

Never you mind for now.
I'll answer that soon enough. Or perhaps I'll get you to answer it.
But first, I need to answer the question you should have asked... Do you know what that might be?

Vincent

No Roxy. I'm not a mind reader.

Roxy

Actually you are – and a pretty good one by all accounts.

Vincent

Well, thank you Roxy. I was wondering when I was going to get a little recognition, and feel the love.

Roxy

Yes, love. It's the highest vibration in the universe.
And I love passing it on.
Especially its most powerful form. Tough love.
I have plenty of that for you.

Vincent

Gee thanks.
It's so reassuring to know I have all that tough love to look forward to. Not.

Now where were we?

Roxy

One little complement and you totally lose your mind. Humans!

You asked a question and I told you there was another one for you to ask me first.

Vincent

So what was that question?

Roxy

... because Mr. Great Mind Reader who lapped up the complements then suddenly lost the ability to read my mind?

(sighs and rolls eyes)

OK. What do we get when we're in the flow?

Vincent

What do we get when we're in the flow?

Roxy

Ah then, life is magical.

Do you believe in magic?

(sigh)

I know, I know. You humans don't any more do you?
You don't notice it and appreciate it when it does turn up in your lives, so you think it simply doesn't exist. And you just pay it lip service, even when it happens to you like it happened at Uluru.

When you're in the flow ...
Powerful suggestions just occur to you as if some ghost whispered directly into your head.

Events magically align so that what was not possible suddenly becomes possible – like your flight to the Northern Territory; and like the unseasonal mild weather when you were expecting baking desert heat, day in day out.

In the flow, everything starts happening in perfect timing. Sometimes it takes a while and sometimes it's near-instantaneous. Either way, it's perfect.

You drive out of the National Park after having visited all the sights, just as it's closing up. Perfect timing.

People want you to work for them and pay you money.

You meet people – old acquaintances, new friends, and those people who you met years ago and totally forgot about, but they remembered you.

You're able to create powerfully. Quickly. Easily.

That's what the flow is like. It's magical.

What outcomes can we expect?

Vincent

So what do we get when we're in it? What outcomes can we expect?

Roxy

Well, Vincent, it's like that kayaking you've done that you have so much fun with.

Now you know you could choose to sit on the bank have a barbecue, decide it's all too much like hard work, call the support team and check out whenever they eventually turn up. And a lot of you humans do the equivalent of that in your lives.

Or you can take a look at the rapids, stop in the shallows and carry your kayak around. It's a lot of work but it's safe.

Or you can just get in the flow and let the current take you through the rapids and, sure, you have to be present to obstacles and avoid them, steer and paddle a wee bit. Just let the river do the hard work. That's the metaphor.

It's fun. It's a delight. And you get to go where the river takes you.

> **Key insight:**
> Getting into the flow makes your life easy and magical, like being carried down a river in a kayak.

What is true Freedom?

Vincent

So you don't have a choice? You have to go down river? Where's the freedom in that?

Roxy

Humans!
How do you define freedom? Freedom of speech? Not having to work? Being able to travel where you want when you want? Being able to vote for someone to represent you in the government – only to be disappointed when they turn out to be – or turn into – a politician.

True freedom lies in becoming the greatest possible version of who you are, not who anybody else is, not who anybody wants you to be. The problem is, most of you humans have no conception of how great you could be and how rewarding that is.

Vincent

But there are so many teachers out there spreading the word about living life on purpose and creating "from your why". Why don't we get it? Or worse still, ignore it?

Roxy

First, like I said, most of you humans have no conception of how great you could be. From the time you were little, you've been told, 'little children should be seen and not heard'. You have been trained and corrected into believing how small you are.

And then, if you do get a subtle sense of your greatness, you discover that stepping into it has a price. It's a small one in the greater scheme of things but it has to be paid up front. It may be giving up your comfortable corporate salary. It may mean spending money on trainings or workshops. It may mean devoting hour after hour to projects that are true for you – with no guarantee of worldly success. And hardest of all is vulnerability – opening yourself up to judgment and criticism.

You're paying that price as you write this book, Vincent, and you have no guarantee of worldly success. Paying that price is uncomfortable for most of you humans. So you try to ignore it and pretend it's not even an option. And then, as you come to the end of your lives, your number one regret is that you didn't have the courage to pay the price, to live a life true to yourself, and instead lived the life others expected of you.

Humans!

> **Key insight:**
> True freedom comes from living a life true to yourself, your innate knowing, your purpose, and true potential; and from letting go of living the life others expect of you.

Summary and next questions.

Roxy

Now, Vincent, perhaps you can sum up what you've learnt in this chapter.
After all, you're pretty smart. For a human.

I wouldn't have come to work with you otherwise,

Vincent

What we learned in this chapter is that there is a universal energetic flow and, when you align with it, life suddenly gets into the flow. It's magical, easier, less stressful and requires much less effort.

But we humans are not prepared to pay the small price of aligning to it.

Roxy

Good enough

Vincent

So why's the universe being so helpful?

Roxy

You humans are so awfully suspicious. Exceptionally suspicious. So lacking in trust.

I'll explain in the next chapter.

Chapter 6

What do you really want?

Flow Posse, what do you want?

Roxy

Hmmm. Why is the universe so helpful?
Well, before we can answer that question, first we have to ask ... Flow Posse, what do you really want?

(brief pause)

Oh my goodness people – just make a mental note of the top highlights. Please!
This is not a journaling exercise. We're not trying to get an exhaustive list of everything you've ever wanted from a new Tesla to climbing Everest to getting a cleaner in once a week. If you really got into it, if you were really super honest, you'd be here till Christmas and beyond. Now just take a moment to make a mental note of your shortlist.

(pause)

What do you humans really want?

OK, you have your shortlist. Now let's move on.

Vincent, I know you've done the work to know this, at least at the level you can handle for now.

But what do you think most people really want in life?

Vincent

Well the easiest way to answer that one is to understand what Maslow said in his hierarchy of needs.

Roxy

You think I'm impressed?

You talk about Maslow and the academic theory as if you're saying, 'Look at me. I've got an MBA?'

Come on – give me something specific. If you gave one of you fellow humans one wish, what would they ask for?

Vincent

To win the lottery?

Roxy

Now that would be right. That seems to be all you humans want to do. Win that vision-board highlighted, prayer-answering, life-changing lottery. It doesn't matter how much money you have. Whether you're a pauper or have piles of money, all you humans seem to wish for is, as you say, 'to win that f***ing lottery'.

Now we're getting somewhere.

That's one of your top wishes isn't it? How did you go last week?

Vincent

You asked me before. You know the answer. Why are you asking me again?

Roxy

(rolls eyes)

Just trust me. I do not ask these questions for fun. Anyway, you didn't give me a straight answer last time. So, please, just answer the question.

Vincent

Well, I didn't win anything.

Roxy

I'm not trying to rub it in, but, do you ever? Or at least, win more than what you spent on the ticket?

But I'll spare you any more embarrassment. We'll move on. What else do humans want?

Vincent

Not looking soooo fat. While eating whatever they want whenever they want without gaining weight.

Roxy

(Rolls her eyes Again.)

That's also one of yours, isn't it?

Of course that's so possible. It's just that none of you humans have figured out how yet. I'll help you write the book, Vincent. It's about the fifth in the series we'll be writing together. Oh Vincent, I didn't tell you, we have a lot of work to do together, did I? You'll just have to get used to working with me.

So, Flow Posse, you're going to have to wait a while for the answers to that one.

Vincent

I just look at food and I put on weight. The doctor keeps nagging me to lose some.

Roxy

You look at food and you put on weight? Do you seriously expect me to believe that? Some time, you should try not picking it up and stuffing it in your mouth. That might just help you get different results.

So this is another thing you want isn't it, Vincent.

But you're just going to have to wait.

What next? If humans had a third wish, what would it be?

Vincent

More sex, better sex.

Roxy

That's about the first half-sensible item on the list. It's what you humans want but won't admit to – most of you anyway. Moreover, it's essential for the survival of your species.

This is another one of yours, isn't it?

Vincent

Yes.

Roxy

How are you going to get that when you don't have a girlfriend?[3]

OK, OK that was a rhetorical question. Spare me the details.

What else do humans want?

Vincent

A big house. A nice car, perhaps a red sports car. Perhaps a luxury vehicle with a sunroof that can parallel park itself. Perhaps a Tesla that yells 'I'm an environmentalist and you're killing the planet'. Whatever a nice car means for them. Smart clothes too. And accessories. Never overlook the accessories, they're so important. Essential. And plenty of money.

Roxy

Stuff. All the "good stuff". All the "right stuff".

---

3   Roxy says

At the time of writing, Vincent did indeed not have a girlfriend. He did though have a fantasy around becoming a world-famous and extremely rich author so, it's entirely possible that, by the time you read this, he has met his soulmate. Perhaps he'll have a drop-dead gorgeous trophy wife. Most likely he'll still be looking. But that's **no excuse** for stalking him on social media.

All the stuff you can't take with you when you go.

> **Key insight:**
>
> **According to Vincent, what most humans want the most is;**
> 1. to win the lottery,
> 2. not look sooo fat while eating whatever they want,
> 3. more sex, better sex, and all the cool stuff you can't take with you when you go.

Why do you humans want what you want?

No, no, no.

What you humans want is mostly wrong.

Let's try this...

Tell me about a program, name a program on TV, the first one that comes to mind.

Vincent

OMG, like *Married at First Sight*?

Roxy

You watch that? Seriously?

That?

Vincent

No. I keep seeing the promos and they're sooo irritating. They're the most annoying promos on TV. I hate them. But I do know lots of people who love that show.

Roxy

>I was hoping for a program that's aspirational, not desperational.
>
>You humans are so desperate for love that some of you will even get married to the first person that comes along. Now this is reality TV so their new spouse will be preselected to look dazzlingly sexy.
>
>And they forget this is reality TV so their new spouse will be preselected to be totally dysfunctional. Where else is the drama going to come from?
>
>Love is indeed wonderful; but trying to find it from lack is so wrong.
>
>*Married at First Sight* is not a bad show.
>
>Actually, it's terrible,
>But it's not bad in the sense of hurting people. I'm not judgmental. But it's simply out of alignment with what you came into this life for as a soul in a physical existence.

> **Key insight:**
> Most of what you humans want comes from a place of lack and neediness, not a place that's aligned with your true purpose and potential.

>And why might that be?

Succeeding at society's roadmap

>You see, you humans have been given a roadmap for the ideal, successful life.
>
>Go to school as soon as you can – and not going is well-nigh illegal.
>Get yourself off to college (well that's ideal).
>Get a good job where you can earn lots of money and drive an

impressive car.
Buy a mega-mansion with a mammoth mortgage that you'll spend all your life paying off. Go on vacation where you can sit on the beach and try to relax and not think about work even though you cannot go anywhere these days without your mobile phone pinging every 2 seconds and the inbox spilling over and the calls that just keep coming.
Get married. Have kids. Go to church. Save for retirement.
Retire and play golf till the day you need to go into a care home and wait till you die.
How does that sound?

Vincent

Terrible.

Playing golf? I can't imagine anything worse.

(sigh)
I once worked with an office full of golfers.

Roxy

I hope you're not looking for sympathy. Again.

You're right about golf, though. It is not a game you play and never was. It's a game that plays you. It takes you over, possesses you, controls you, turns you into an addict, drains your wallet, deals you untold frustration and misery, day after day after day. And yet you keep coming back for the next fix.

It enslaves everybody it touches – presidents, prime ministers, captains of industry. Some say golf is the public arm of the dark elite of Scotland's plan to gain world domination. Scottish rite freemasonry is the secretive arm and its tentacles suck in the same people.

Supposedly.

But I digress
No, no, no, not the golf.
The roadmap. How does that sound?

Never mind. Another rhetorical question. I know the real answer. Of course.

That's the script you follow. That's the roadmap. You humans have an uneasy feeling or, rather, a deep uneasy knowing, that it's all just a script you've been given and there's something not right with it.

But still, for most of you, your goals and dreams, your desires and ambitions come directly from this roadmap. And society reflects them back – the qualifications, the salary, the cars, the houses, the money, the exotic vacations, the trophy spouses, the private jets, the high achieving kids and so on and so on.

> **Key insight:**
> Most of you humans follow the roadmap that's created for you by society. It sets you humans up to fail in life – whether or not you succeed by the rules of your society's roadmap.

Are you feeling like a failure?

Vincent

Who? Me?

Roxy

Well who else is in this conversation?

Humans!

Vincent

I often feel like an underachiever.

But not everybody follows this roadmap.

Roxy

I said you humans have a word for them. Failures

Roadmaps for the religious and spiritual

Vincent

> But what about the people who choose to be monks or nuns, who work in the community or meditate in a monastery in the remote reaches of the Himalayas?

Roxy

> As you humans have been given a roadmap for an ideal life, so you then have to apply a dismissive label to those people who choose not to follow it.
>
> You call them eccentrics, weirdos, hippies.
>
> MAYBE they do good work but they're not normal. They've been "taken by the cult".
>
> You humans judge them. Perhaps you grudgingly acknowledge that, in some way, they're doing something – SOMETHING to make the world a better place.
>
> Now maybe sometimes you'll buy a recording of the Dalai Lama or one of those Osho card decks you see everywhere, because you can't be truly spiritual if you don't have an Osho deck; or some meditation tracks. Perhaps you'll sponsor a kid in Africa. But you wouldn't choose to go so far as to create your life like those weirdo people would you? It may be all well and good to spend a gap year in their communities and ashrams but come on, take on that lifestyle seriously?
>
> I mean, Vincent, would you become a monk or a nun? No you couldn't become a nun – well in what you humans call these modern times, even that's possible, but would you choose to take up poverty as a way of life?
>
> As opposed to creating it for yourself by, well, LET'S BE KIND, YOUR OWN LIMITING BELIEFS AND POOR JUDGMENT.

Vincent

> No – I wouldn't choose poverty.

Roxy

There's a bible story about a rich young man who asks Jesus what he must do to gain eternal life. So Jesus asks, 'Are you obeying the commandments' and the man says, 'Yes and what else can I do?'[4]

Now at that point Jesus could have just said 'Don't give me that bullshit'.
I would have; with love, of course. Tough love.

Obey the commandments? All the time? Oh, come on. Never tells lies? Never covet your neighbor's wife? Take the name of the Lord in vain? That's just what you humans do all the time. It's Old Testament God setting up humans to fail.

But Jesus doesn't do that. No. Instead, he tells the rich young man to sell all his possessions, to give the cash to the poor and come and follow him.

That's Jesus' life roadmap for you humans. But do you see Christians doing it?
And Christians may think that's hard or perhaps they try not to think about it at all; but they should consider themselves lucky, prefer to gloss over that part of Christianity, then they should consider themselves lucky. In Roman times, Christians had to go the extra mile to follow Jesus. It could get them crucified or thrown to the lions.

Would modern-day-Christians be up for Jesus' roadmap? Selling ALL their possessions, mobile phones included, and giving all the money to the poor?

Vincent

Some of the missionaries perhaps? The religious who take a vow of poverty?

Roxy

Sure. And they do great work. No problem with them.

---

4 the Gospel of Matthew 19:16–30, the Gospel of Mark 10:17–31 and the Gospel of Luke 18:18–30

But Christian institutions from the Vatican to the televangelists, they seem to be all about the money. And the sex. I could expound on that for eternity; but we do have to get this book done.

So you have society's roadmap that leads to a life of hard work creating nothing of lasting value which leads you to regrets at the end of your life.

Then you have the demanding roadmaps your spiritual leaders offer and where does that lead you?

Vincent

Salvation? Eternal life? A prime spot in heaven when we die? Staying out of hell and the fire and brimstone?

Roxy

Or, for those of you who believe in reincarnation, coming back as something marginally better than a cockroach.

And while you deny yourself and live a life of poverty, what's happening with the leaders who are selling that lifestyle? How many Rolls Royces did Osho have before he left the USA? How poor is the Vatican?

It's all a bit rich isn't it.

You see, I started this chapter with the question, 'what do you really want?'; and most of you humans have absolutely no clue what the true answer is to that question because it's hidden so deeply under your layers of wounding and social conditioning.

> **Key insight:**
> Most you humans have no idea what you truly want because it's hidden under layers of wounding and social conditioning.

A better roadmap – your meaning and purpose.

Vincent

So how do we even find out what we really want?

Roxy

It's simple and easy. Seriously.

Each of you has come to this planet with a purpose and a potential so great you can't comprehend it, your true potential. That purpose is aligned with the universe. It's available for you from your intuition – if only you humans would stop, admit you're all innately intuitive; or, better, claim your intuitive gifts; and listen to what your intuition tells you. What you get will be right for you. What you're aiming for. Where you're going. What action you need to take. What outcomes are right for you in this life. You have only to tune in to it.[5]

Vincent

That sounds wonderful. And it sounds easy enough. What's the catch?

Roxy

The catch is that your society has done an effective job of getting you humans to tune out you intuition. Society makes you think all the time. It makes you mental. And that blocks the intuitive flow. So, while you humans have amazing intuitive skills, for most of you, it's blocked and you've lost access to the information that's out there that's truly important for you.

What do you do instead, you live by the unconscious rules that come from your childhood wounding; and from the roadmap society has given you. Those rules govern your life.

---

[5] Roxy says … and if you're asking how you can have all this? … Humans! You are so impatient, always seeking instant gratification. We will cover this later in the book.

Summary .

We'll unpack this some more soon enough but first, please would you sum up?

Vincent

Hmmm. All of us humans have a long list of things we want in life.

But it turns out we don't really want them. We just think we do. And those thoughts are the result of our core wounding and social conditioning.

We can uncover what we really want in life through using our intuition and we will get to that soon enough.

> **Key insight:**
> You can uncover what you truly desire in life through using your intuition. You will learn processes for this as you journey through this book.

Roxy

Yes. Did I rant a bit in that chapter?

Vincent

You did.

Roxy

Thank goodness. Whatever it takes to get the message across. With love. Tough love.

Chapter 7

The seductive power of your comfort zone

Intuition will tell us what we want – so why don't we get it?

Vincent

    In the last chapter we learned that we can find out what we really want in life through intuition.

    But there are plenty of intuition teachers around.

    Why don't more people get it? Why isn't the word out on the grapevine 'get intuitive, find what makes you truly happy'? Why isn't it a powerful movement sweeping the world?

Roxy

    But Vincent, you know the answer. What is it?

Vincent

    Is it because the teachers are lousy at marketing?

Roxy

    That's what they'll tell you. And they certainly have room for improvement. A lot of room.

    It's not the answer though.

Vincent

    Then is it because the teachers sabotage themselves?

Roxy

> Of course they do; and far more than you think.
> And I do include you in that as well.
> You are indeed super-creative when it comes to sabotage.
>
> But that is not the answer either.

Vincent

> Is it because the teachers are boring?

Roxy

> Do you consider yourself to be boring?

Vincent

> Well, to be honest, I'm sure we all can be – at least from time to time.

Roxy

> I'll take that as a yes; and that's as maybe. I won't judge you for it though.
>
> But whatever makes you think that, when people don't use their intuition to decide what they want in life, it has to be the fault of your intuition teachers for not being good enough?

Vincent

> Surely you're not blaming it on our students? Or the people who choose not to listen?

The guilty secret of the comfort zone

Roxy

> Actually, for once, I am.
>
> You see the problem with you humans is that most of you live in a comfort zone.
>
> Comfort zone. That's a misnomer if ever there was one.

Because it's often most uncomfortable in your comfort zone. You're frequently unhappy there. Thoreau was right. Most of you humans do indeed live lives of quiet desperation[7].

> **Key insight:**
> Most humans live lives of quiet desperation

But you have a guilty secret.

Vincent

That makes it sound like we humans are criminals. Like a murderer in a detective show. They always have a guilty secret that turns out to be the motive for their crime.

Roxy

Exactly. You humans are criminal. It's criminal how you let your lives slip away without really living. It's as if you're murdering yourselves with a slow-acting but inexorable poison.

Why?

Would you mind if I do my Poirot impression, it's so perfect for exposing the guilty secret?

Vincent

If you must. As if I can stop you.

The dread of leaving your comfort zone

Roxy

Merci. You see, you humans have a guilty secret. Oh yes.

You sense at a deep level how wonderful life could be if you

---

6   Roxy says ... yes, most humans does include Vincent for much of his life
7   Henry David Thoreau – Walden – 1864. The original quote reads "The mass of men lead lives of quiet desperation."

were only to step outside that comfort zone. What adventures you could have. What amazing people you could meet. How fulfilling your life could be.... But no. You will not countenance that.

Non.

The very thought of stepping outside your comfort zone fills you with dread. With terror. It activates each and every fear and unconscious belief you have and those beliefs ring alarm bells, fortissimo like Quasimodo at the Cathédrale de Notre Dame. The slightest thought of stepping outside your comfort zone lights up your wounding. It activates all manner of pain and emotion. If you set a foot outside your comfort zone, you very rapidly pull it back in at even the slightest hint of adversity.

That, Vincent, that is the guilty secret you humans share. You are more comfortable staying inside your comfort zone than taking even a single step outside

That is what leads you to bestow upon yourselves a slow uncomfortable death by simply passing up on the opportunity to truly live.

Vincent

That's really sad.

Sorry, I didn't mean your Poirot impression – that was fantastic

No, the message you deliver is so sad.

Roxy

Oh yes. I know it's sad. And it shows up at the end of your lives, when you are no longer able to do anything about it. You even have wonderful books like Bronnie Ware's 'The Top Five Regrets of the Dying' which tell you this. On your deathbeds, you humans wish you'd had the courage to live a life true to yourself, not the life you believed others expected of you.

But, by then, it's too late.

Humans!

> **Key insight:**
> Most of you humans are terrified of stepping out of your comfort zones. Then, on your deathbeds, you regret that you didn't live a life true to yourselves and instead lived the life you believed others expected of you.

Vincent

So can you help me and the Flow Posse understand a little deeper about why we prefer being uncomfortable in our comfort zone to stepping out?

Why is stepping outside the comfort zone so uncomfortable?

Roxy

Well, Vincent, you see magic and flow happening in your life. Right now, you see it several times a week. This week, you've had two group calls where only one other person came and yet, both times, you had deep conversations that helped you on your path. Last week, the joy of teaching intuition to a much younger group than you have had before. The week before, a message out of the blue from a friend who had offered to help you with this book when you hadn't heard from her for a while. Even the way you received a recommendation to the perfect publisher when you weren't even looking.

You're training yourself to notice it and record it. Very good VG. You don't see everything but you do see the highlights as they happen. It's really unexpected and driven by coincidence and synchronicity. It's normal for you – and the people you work with. You love it.

But for most modern humans, that's not the case. It makes them uncomfortable. They have been told that the world is mostly random so they assume that everything is random. That saves them from having to observe magic when it happens.

They screen it out. They don't notice it. And if they do see something that's unusual, they try to ignore it. These days, many of you even ask, 'how random is that?' as if everything has to be random to some extent. You had an email today with the subject 'Random question …' as if there was no real intent when the author wrote it.

Magic and flow scares most humans when it happens because it upsets your view of a random world. Am I right or am I right?

Vincent

Well of course you're right. You always are. And you know that. I don't know why you bother asking me.

Roxy

Oh but you do know why I'm asking you. My question was not a random question. So thank you for answering and I'll continue …

Although most of you have a fear of magic and flow, from time to time, you humans do experience an extraordinary synchronicity, often when you're kept safe from serious injury or even death. Perhaps you go to cross the road and at the last minute, someone yells out and you stop and a truck speeds by. That's a big shock to you. But you put it all down to randomness.

No. Randomness is being hit by the truck.

Synchronicity is when you're saved at the last second by a stranger who just happened to be there and within earshot and able to call out the warning in a way that caught your attention.

> **Key insight:**
> Most of you humans hold an entrenched belief that reality is totally random. That's why you can't see synchronicities and other forms of magic when they happen.

Why are society's beliefs so entrenched?

If you humans were to acknowledge that magic did work, it would be frightening for you. Your whole world view would have to change and you humans are so resistant to change. In the Middle Ages and Renaissance times, you followed what the pope said as the truth of how the world is. From time to time, usually after decades, he would change the church's dogma to align with some new view of reality that science had revealed and was undeniable. The earth is round. The earth goes around the sun and not vice versa.

But in modern times, your communal beliefs are entrenched not with one person but through the whole society like a big oak tree with roots that spread wide and deep; and that makes it so much more difficult to change. You have to persuade not one but millions of people that a particular change in viewpoint is real and valid.

Vincent

You make it sound like it's impossible to change society's viewpoint.

Can humans adopt new ideas as quickly as we adopted smartphones?

Roxy

Not exactly. It's easy if enough of you make it attractive enough, desirable enough. Look how quickly the humans embraced smart phones. Surely you can make it attractive and desirable to embrace living from your inner truth and intuition? Or am I expecting too much from humans?

Vincent

Perhaps you are.

Roxy

No I'm not. If you humans can embrace smart phones in a few

short years, why not living purposeful, rewarding, fulfilled and happy lives?

Now remember, back in the 60s you had Star Trek and the crew had little hand-held communication device with which they could talk to their spacecraft orbiting the planet. Then, it seemed like science fiction. Since the late 2000s you've had devices that not only allow you to not only communicate – audio AND video but also read books, tune your guitar, buy whatever you want and even check where the cheapest gas is near you.

How much more desirable would a truly happy life be for you humans?

Vincent

I think given a choice between true happiness and a smartphone, humans would ...

Roxy

Did I say it was an either/or choice? I don't think I did – thankfully for you humans there is no reason you can't have both and there is no reason why a big spiritual shift can't come equally quickly.

Why humans fear magical success

However, there is yet another reason that you humans reject magic and flow. It's that you humans might actually be successful in your lives.

Imagine that! Then you might behave too sheepishly to admit to others that you were using what you call "woo woo" rather than working hard and battling your way through obstacles and challenges. Perhaps you might be landed with responsibilities that you fear you can't handle. Perhaps you fear being overwhelmed with so much to do. Perhaps you might have so much money you become a magnet for thieves.

The illusion of comfort in the comfort zone

So you choose life in the comfort zone. And you choose to try to make it as comfortable as possible with distractions and comforts and entertainment and busyness. And the more you make your comfort zone more comfortable for the mind and body the less comfortable it becomes for the spirit. And so the quiet desperation continues.

You all know you have the innate potential to live from and in your greatness. You all know that would lead you to live a life true to yourself and even one that's inspirational and fabulous. You all know that, on your deathbeds, you'd be perfectly happy with no regrets whatsoever. And yet you prefer to stay in that comfort zone.

Even though it's less rewarding.

Even though it leads you to a life partner, attracted not by your dreams but by your shared emotional wounding.

Even though it's a more painful way to live.

And even though on your deathbed, you will regret it all. You will regret not stepping out of your comfort zone. You'll wish you'd done it. But it's all too late.

So why won't you step outside your comfort zone in life? Because you're addicted to the pain there. You're used to it, and probably have been since childhood. And you simply assume life outside has to be more painful.

How do we persuade more humans to take that step?

Vincent

I live out of my comfort zone – and there have been scary times but it has also been amazing. But how do we persuade others to take that step?

Roxy

Very good question, VG.

You see there are two steps to stepping outside your comfort zone. Ironic isn't it – you have to take steps to step outside your comfort zone.

Step 1 is simply to understand and accept that you are in a comfort zone. Imagine a fish living in a fish bowl. Does it know it's living in water? No! It has no idea because it will never experience being outside of water. That's what you humans are like. Your comfort zone is your equivalent of the fish's bowl. It's a boundary you don't cross. However, unlike fish, you do have the capacity to see your comfort zone for what it is.

And when you do, when you realize what an illusion it is, you see the comfort zone as a scary place that's running your life and keeping you from making the most of it.

Step 2 is to understand that there is a way out of the comfort zone that is powerful and rewarding. I will unpack that when we talk about alignment.

You can't persuade everybody, Vincent. However, many of you humans are open to it now. There will still be humans who want to ignore it, relax into quiet desperation, and numb themselves with Netflix. We have to allow them their free will. This is not for them.

But many of you are waking up and feeling that there's more to life. You are the people we can influence in this book. You are the Flow Posse.

> **Key insight:**
> Most humans don't realize that they live life in their comfort zone and that they have the option of stepping out.
>
> Once you realize you're in a comfort zone, it's simple to step out (but not necessarily easy!).

The Universe is ready to help

And when you do step out of your comfort zone and into your aligned life journey, the universe is standing there ready to give you a profound sense of your mission, purpose, and true potential; and help you build a great life that serves yourself and others powerfully. We will come to how you find that aligned life journey and take action on it later in the book.

Now, Vincent, please would you summarize.

Summary

Vincent

Most of us humans live in our comfort zones, even though we know that the comfort is an illusion. We dread the idea of stepping out, partly because of what might befall us and mostly because of how we'll be judged. Once we get past our fears, stepping out of the comfort zone and into alignment is an empowering experience.

Chapter 8

Why should the universe help us, anyway?

Why should the universe care?

Vincent

> So what we've established so far is that staying in the comfort zone is a bad idea and that getting into the flow is basically a good one...

Roxy

> That's an understatement if ever there was one. Carry on.

Vincent

> Can you let me finish my sentence?

Roxy

> Don't you get that attitude with me Vincent. I don't have to spend my eternity trying to educate you – it's like trying to teach the fleas in a circus new tricks.
>
> I assure you, I would not interject unless it was important for our Flow Posse.

Vincent

> No no no. Not a moody muse.

Roxy

> I heard that. You want moody? I'll give you moods. Multidimensional and nuclear moods. It's all part of the love. If

you find yourself on the receiving end of them, it's because you need some tough love.

So now remind me, or rather remind our Flow Posse – why is it so important to get out of their comfort zone and get into the flow?

Vincent

To experience the joy and fulfillment of living life on-purpose and to receive those synchronicities, chance meetings, perfect timing, opportunities that seem to come from nowhere. Anything that will help us create our end results with greater ease. That's why.

Roxy

Good.

Vincent

(sigh)

Thanks. Are we good now?

Roxy

I'm always good but are you? Get on with it, what's the next question?

Vincent

So why does the universe even care?

And if it does care, why doesn't it help all the time?

Roxy

Why does the universe care?

Who says it cares?

Tell me, how did the universe start out?

Vincent

Well, it was like a big ball of incandescent gas that kind of exploded into being.

Roxy

A big ball of gas?

Vincent

Actually, it wasn't big was it – microscopic and super super heavy.

Roxy

Well, that is the kindergarten version but it will do for now. Good.

And how is the universe now?

Vincent

It's big.

Roxy

Big? You call a family size pizza big. Big like that?

Vincent

Well, ginormous. Like, it would take many human lifetimes to cross it. Do you want me to look up how many Olympic size swimming pools big it is? Calculate how many family-size pizzas you'd have to lay end to end to get across it?

Roxy

Be careful what you ask for, Vincent. I might just say yes.

The universe is expanding

So how did it get like that?

Vincent

There was the big bang like a mega explosion and it's been expanding ever since.

Roxy

What was that you said?

Vincent

Surely you got it the first time.

I said there was the big bang like a mega explosion and it's been expanding ever since.

Roxy

Vincent, there is a reason I repeat questions. You know the answers. I know you know the answers. You know I know you know the answers. I'm not stupid, even though you often treat me that way.

Humans!

However, those answers sometimes need repeating to really sink in. For emphasis. So that our Flow Posse really understands how important that is.

So the universe is expanding is it?

Vincent

That's what I said. Twice. Why are you playing deaf?

Roxy

Why are you playing dumb?
That's the point. The universe is expanding. That's important. That's key. The universe is expanding. That's just how it is. That's its nature.

> **Key insight:**
> The universe is expanding. That's its nature.

Now, next question.

What's the earth made up of?

Vincent

All sorts of minerals and clays and sand and oceans and rivers.

Roxy
And life?

Vincent
Yes. Plants and animals and birds and insects and microbes.

Roxy
And was all that stuff there at the big bang?

Vincent
No. Like I said, it was all a microscopic but hugely dense sea of subatomic particles.

Roxy
Was it now? Well, you're still passing kindergarten Quantum Mechanics... Nothing more than I'd expect mind you[8].

Although if you ask the average human in the street ...
They will probably think Schrödinger's cat was the one on the divine gourmet salmon flavored pet food ads.
Schrödinger missed a money-making opportunity there.

So how did all those subatomic particles become the earth with its rocks and sands and water and life?

Vincent
I don't know.

Roxy
Vincent! One minute you're accusing me of asking dumb questions and the next minute you're giving me dumb answers. As if you don't know. You do.

---

8   Roxy says
Vincent's first degree was a B.Tech in Applied Chemistry. He thinks he still remembers something from the Quantum Mechanics he studied at that time, and he may just be right – even though it was thirty, no, forty, no ... many years ago. As I once guided Alexander Pope to write, 'A little knowledge is a dangerous thing'. So you can make your own minds up as to how dangerous Vincent's knowledge of this area is.

So we'll play a little game. If you did know the answer, what would it be?

Vincent

Evolution?

The universe is evolving

Roxy

Evolution? Like the survival of the fittest? Like which is the fittest – a proton, a neutron or electron?

However, you are close.

The universe is always creating, exploring, experimenting. And this activity is how it evolved. First it was just the basic natural elements. Then chemical compounds, gases, liquids, and solids like the rocks.

Then life – microbes, algae, plants. Up and up to animals, mammals and, finally intelligent life – you humans.

Ok, that's going a wee bit far. Let's just say, ah, semi-intelligent life. There were lots of blind alleys too. Some things didn't work out. Some creatures and plants only survive in certain conditions and when there's a climate change then they're gone – like the dinosaur extinction after that big meteorite hit the Gulf of Mexico and caused the planet to cool.

> **Key insight:**
> The universe is evolving. That's also its nature.

The universe is creating

But the universe is always creating through whatever system is available to it. It's creating through you humans right now. Nations, societies, cities, works of art, and scientific discoveries.

Do you get that?

Vincent

Yes. So why is the universe always creating?

Roxy

I don't know. We don't know the why. We don't need to know why.

It just is.

It's like why do elephants have trunks?

Vincent

Is it because they'd look silly with glove compartments?

Roxy

I think it may be best if I do the jokes from here.

Now you could Google why elephants have trunks and be on the end of ads for expensive luxury safaris for the next couple of weeks and you might even get a serious answer.
Or, you could just say it doesn't matter why elephants have trunks. That's just how they are, and they have turned them into very effective tools.

Vincent

They're awesome. I've seen them use their trunks to give themselves showers when it's hot.

Roxy

It sounds cool, even though I find it difficult to relate. I never shower.

You can't tell though, can you?

Of course not...

So the universe is always creating. It's inherently creative. Now you're part of the universe that's inherently creative so you're inherently creative too.

Do you get that?

> **Key insight:**
> The universe is inherently creative. That's its nature.

Vincent

I think so.

Roxy

It's simple enough. Of course you get it and of course you then let your dumb yourself down to try and make out that you don't. Why? Humans!

So when you get the urge to build a house or paint a picture or write a song, you're being creative and your inner creativity is coming through. So far so good?

Vincent

Yes.

The universe creates through you

Roxy

Because when you are creating something like that, you are super-aligned with the universe and the same forces that created the elements and molecules and rocks and oceans and life and even supposedly intelligent humans – you're aligned with those forces and they come in and help you. The universe creates through you.

So what was that question you asked earlier?

Vincent

Why do elephants have trunks?

Roxy

I said I'd do the jokes. And it was me that asked that question.

I have a memory like an elephant. Actually it's infinitely bigger and far cleverer but that's just what you humans say.

No, the original question at the start of this chapter.

> **Key insight:**
> The universe creates through you.

Why does the universe care?

Vincent

Why does the universe even care? And if it does care, why doesn't it help all the time?

Roxy

Did I say the universe cared?

(pauses)

Well, did I?

Vincent

No, you didn't.

Roxy

So what did I say?

Vincent

You said that the universe is inherently creative, we're part of the universe and so we're all inherently creative. And so when we – as part of the universe – we go to create something the universe lines up with us and we piggy-back on that alignment like a kayak in a river current.

> **Key insight:**
> The universe doesn't care if you align with its essential creativity or not. It's your free choice.

So what's the catch

Roxy

Very good, VG.

So, I hear you say, because I'm telepathic – did I tell you that? I hear you say there's got to be a catch. And you're right. There's a big one. You have to be truly creative. Creating something new and novel and expansive. Expansive that is, not expensive. The higher the level of your creativity, the more the universe steps in to help you.

If you're creating something destructive like world war 3, the universe won't kick in. But the universe won't stand in your way either. Some people call it free will. It is. It's just an allowing of all possibilities.

Vincent

So how do you measure how creative you're being? Whether you're creating a masterpiece or total destruction? Something that's in the middle or... or... something you believe is a masterpiece but actually is garbage?

Roxy

That's a powerful question, one I'm sure the Flow Posse will want an answer to.

So how do you measure how creative you're being? You feel it intuitively. If it flows out of you, if it has freshness, if it feels beautiful, then it's high-level creativity, If it feels forced, it's not flowing, if every little step is hard work, then it's not creative. Understand?

> **Key insight:**
> When you're being truly creative, you have an innate knowing that you are and you sense it intuitively.

Summary

Vincent

Yes

So when you're in a high level of creativity, you're helped along by the universe because you're in its energetic flow of expansion, evolution and creation. How's that for a summary

Roxy

Very good, VG. That's simple but powerful. Let's move on.

Part 3

Understanding the flow

Chapter 9

Alignment

Getting started the flow - Alignment

Vincent

So if getting into the flow is so important, what do we need to know about getting started?

Roxy

It's very simple, Vincent. First, you have to align with it. That's all.

Vincent

Isn't that what some people do? They sit on the couch and feeling in the vibration of abundance and visualizing vast sums of money coming to them? Like coins spilling out of a slot machine or bank bills fluttering down like snow.

What's wrong with that?

Roxy

Oh, but did I say there was anything wrong with it? I think you'll find not. After all, I'm never judgmental and I'm not going to make this into a moral judgment.

It's just a monumental waste of time.

> **Key insight:**
> Just visualizing what you want won't attract it to you.

Now for me as an eternal spirit being, that's never a problem. I have all of eternity. And I don't have to eat, sleep, rave, repeat and do everything else that you humans do. But for you, you have to attend to the basics of living in a physical world.

You are mortal beings. You're going to die. I know you don't like to think about it so you all agree to suppress the thought and consider it unrefined to talk about it. Meanwhile, your unconscious is continually reminding you, 'you're going to die, better get on with that bucket list and make sure you wear clean underwear when you go out' and loading you down with a host of similar demands.

You're physical beings. You need food and shelter. And a mobile phone – and not necessarily in that order. And you have to work at providing those for yourself. You don't have all day to sit around on the couch visualizing piles of money coming to you and let me remind you, even if you did, it would not do any good.

Vincent

Why not?

Roxy

Can't you just take my word for it? I said I'm a powerful cosmic multidimensional megabeing. Are you not able to just listen?

Vincent

Oh come on Roxy. I know you're all that stuff. I work with you every day.

Roxy

Work? You call this work? You're a lazy good for nothing layabout. Actually no. Busy, overwhelmed, yes. A true hive of inessential activity? Absolutely! Plagued by resistance that distracts you from working? Definitely. Lazy? Well, actually, not often – but you might as well be.

Vincent

But the Flow Posse, they won't get it...

Roxy

Oh yes – your readers. Will they ever get it?

(Pauses)

OK, I'll answer the question at the level our Flow Posse will be able to understand. Are you sitting comfortably?

Vincent

This is not *"Listen with Mother?"*[1].

Roxy

Well, it is kindergarten level. And you need it.

And don't forget, you are not as smart as you think. You're the one who thought you deleted this part of the conversation and made me do this section all over again. Then you realized that what you thought you'd deleted was there all along.

Humans!

Recap - how did the universe start out?

OK let's recap. How did the universe start out?

Vincent

It was a big ball of gas. Actually no – more like a small but very dense soup of subatomic particles. And then it exploded in what we call the big bang. A mega explosion; and it's been expanding ever since.

---

1   Roxy says -
Listen with Mother was a fifteen minute-long daily BBC radio program which Vincent listened to as a pre-schooler because his father wouldn't let the family have television.

Roxy

> Close enough for kindergarten-level. We agree that the universe has created atoms, molecules, stars, planets, rocks and water, plants, microbes, birds, animals, and mosquitos. That's a lot of things that the universe has created.

How much money it cost to create the universe?

> So how much money did all that cost?

Vincent

> The universe didn't need money to create all that.

Roxy

> Really? The universe didn't need money? You astonish me! I would never have guessed.

Vincent

> I give you a right answer and all I get back is attitude with a dollop of sarcasm.

Roxy

> And love. Tough love. I promise you it's all for dramatic effect.
>
> So do you think the universe is really worried or concerned about money?

Vincent

> Of course not.

> **Key insight:**
> The universe does not care about money.

But don't we need money?

> But we humans, we're different aren't we? We need it for stuff – not just survival, not just food and shelter but for all sorts of

stuff, creative, leisure, travel, taxes, whatever. Even us creatives need things like musical instruments, art materials, and we want to create stuff that's really in alignment, like retreat centers, churches, temples. It's essential.

Roxy

Did I say it wasn't useful? No, I did not. If you need money for something creative and expansive – even if it's something like say, a cat grooming business, you're aligned with the universe and it will help you get it.

Needing money is living in lack energy.

But if you're sitting on the couch asking for money, how is that in alignment? What are you creating? How are you expansive? You're not. You're just sending the universe a powerful message that you don't have money and that you're living in lack.

Yes. It's unconscious. You think you're vibrating wealth and abundance but your unconscious is continually pushing you to try harder because you're so poor. You're poor. So poor.

Does the universe look at you sitting on the couch and forcing yourself to be happy and think 'Yes'. And you seem to like sitting comfortably on that couch with lack at the back of your mind, so I'm going to dump more of that lack on you? Or does it just pass you by like a river current flows on past a backwater?

Vincent

It seems to do both.

What would you do if the money came?

Roxy

Exactly. And if the money suddenly did come to you, what would you do with it?

Vincent

    That's a good question.

Roxy

    Of course it is. I asked it.

Vincent

    Well, most people who are sitting on the couch, if they had the money, they'd probably go out and buy a new house and a new car and some new clothes and quit their jobs and head to Hawaii for a week or six.

Roxy

    You wouldn't do that would you?

Vincent

    Actually, I probably would…

Roxy

    I suppose so. You're just a human. It's seductive isn't it? You humans are so easily seduced. And that's another book we'll be doing together…

    However, if a human had the money, they'd have their partner and family and extended family and those members of the extended family they didn't even know existed and their friends, not just the close ones, but the ones that they haven't seen for years and are suddenly bosom buddies, churches, schools charities all asking for help and saying you can afford this now.

    So those lottery winners fritter their money away. After all it's good to be generous. It will get you on the right side of friends and family (watch them disappear when it's all gone). And it will surely get you a nice spot in heaven when you die – great insurance, that.

    In no time, all the money is gone. What's so creative about that?

    Is that aligned with the flow of the universe?

> **Key insight:**
> Many lottery winners fritter their money away, riches to rags. Some even go bankrupt. Winning the lottery is no guarantee of health, wealth, and happiness for life[2].

Vincent

Well you make it sound like it isn't.

Roxy

You are right. Regrettably, that's how it is most of the time with you humans.

It's like you take a kayak out on the river. What's the smart way to go?

Vincent

Downstream of course.

Roxy

Yes. With the current helping you. That's how the universe is.

Imagine that, sitting in a backwater and meditating and visualizing and pleading with the current to come and carry you downstream. Do you think the current would come?

You have to get into the flow.

Vincent

Well no. Obviously not. You have to get your kayak into the current if that's what you want.

---

2 Roxy writes ... The most commonly quoted statistic is that 70% end up broke and a third go on to declare bankruptcy. However, all the best statistics and quotes on the internet are made up and this statistic has been disowned by its supposed source. Nevertheless, anecdotal evidence of the curse of the lottery is easy to find online.

Roxy

Exactly. As if you'd want to sit in a backwater all day till someone comes and rescues you. And wonder why nobody comes.

Suddenly, we have some insight.

In a kayak, you have three options. Go upstream. Sometimes that's useful. For example, if you're a group leader and you need to shepherd the group. Or you use the river as a highway and you want to get back to where you started – assuming there's a way where the current is reasonably gentle. Option two — you can sit in a backwater doing nothing – or even pull the kayak up onto the bank. It's comfortable at least for a while but it's not getting you anywhere. Or option three – you can get into the current and head downstream with the river.

Now which of those seems to make most sense to you? Which is easiest? Which is most fun? Which is in flow?

Vincent

Heading downstream of course.

Roxy

Congratulations! Perhaps you humans may be able to justify considering yourselves to be intelligent life, after all.

So remind me, why are we talking about canoeing?

Vincent

Because it's a metaphor for how the universe works?

Roxy

Exactamente. Perfecto.

Vincent

WTF? Why have you suddenly started speaking Spanish?

Roxy

For emphasis. I love Español – positivo, decisivo

Ahora...

The universe is like a river, like the current in the river. So if you align with it, it helps you. If you don't, well you may occasionally still enjoy some measure of success but you'll have to use a lot more energy, a lot more force.

Comprender?

Vincent

Si.
OMG you've got me talking Spanish now.

Roxy

Bueno – there was a reason you got that term of Spanish in before you changed schools – and a reason why you changed schools but that's another story.

> **Key insight:**
> Aligning with the universe is like paddling a kayak into the flow of a river's current. Once you're there, the current takes you and it takes very little effort to move downstream.

Recap – the nature of the universe.

So what did we establish about the universe?

Vincent

That it's expanding, creating, evolving.

Roxy

Bueno, muy bueno.

So what good does it do sitting on the couch and visualizing all that money coming to you.

Vincent

No good at all.

Roxy

Muy Bueno.

So, perhaps you can help me understand exactly why many of you humans do that?

Vincent

Well, it can be a tough world to live in and some people just want a break.

Roxy

Tough world to live in?

Go back 100 years. They told people smoking was good for your health; people smoked and were extremely lucky to live long enough to retire. Diseases like polio and tuberculosis were everywhere – no cures, no vaccines. And you'd know that. Tuberculosis claimed your grandfather while your father was still in his teens. World War One had not long finished and most families in Europe and many across the rest of the world were left heartbroken and grieving their dead – like your grandmother's family. That was a tough world. Has the world evolved for the better?

Vincent

I suppose so. Now we have the Internet and Tik Tok and mobile phones.

Roxy

But you're not dying so, so young anymore. You have education, you have health services...

Go back only 200 years. Famines, disease. Children expected to work and only the lucky ones escape a miserable cycle of existence. Has the world evolved for the better?

Vincent

I suppose so.

Choosing to align with the evolving universe

Roxy

See, the universe is continually evolving. Your world is continually evolving.

You humans can choose to align with that. And when you are in alignment, it's as if your vision for your life is magnetized to come to you. Or you can choose to sit on the couch and dream of money and visualize it and stay out of alignment.

That's a choice. That's the choice for each of you humans.

And now, more than ever in your history, many of you have the awareness that it's a choice you can make and that you have the opportunity to make that choice.

Look, there's nothing wrong with taking a break from time to time, a café coffee, a week on the beach, a hiking adventure, whatever. In fact, it's good – you humans seem to need that. But a break is a break. Your purpose in life is not to get on the beach at every possible opportunity and get nicely bronzed.

> **Key insight:**
> Aligning with the universe is a choice that each human has.

So why do humans not align?

Vincent

So why do so many humans not align? Why do we have those sorts of goals?

Getting into the Flow

Roxy

You're the human. You should know. But putting it simply, you humans have free will. It's not just about choosing to be good or being naughty, the way they talk about in the churches. Sinful, they call it. And you know who the sinful ones really are – the naughty vicars that the News of the World used to 'expose' week after week after week when it was still being published; pedophile priests, megachurch pastors busted for sexual misconduct; all while telling their congregations how to behave.

No, It's about far more than that. What free will is really about is you having the choice to align with the universe or not. To seek purpose or seek pleasure. To be a creative being in your full power or a couch potato or even world domination. It is free will. It is your choice.

There will of course, be consequences both in your physical world and in the astral, in consciousness whatever you choose. Maybe you'll find those consequences to be desirable, that you'd love and maybe you'd want to run a million miles from them.

Whatever, we higher beings don't judge you.

Vincent

Yes you do. You judge me all the time.

Roxy

No I don't. No we don't. We just have wisdom. And discernment. And love. tough love.

> **Key insight:**
> Humans have free will and can decide whether or not to align with the universe. There's no judgment. However, there are consequences!

How did you come out of alignment?

Another key question is why are you humans not in alignment already? After all, you were in alignment when you were born...

Vincent

Well, it's just life as a human.
It's like wheels on a car. You take it and get them aligned; then drive them around on the local roads with all the bumps and potholes and sure enough, soon enough they're out of alignment again. It just happens. Doesn't it?

Roxy

It's a wee bit more than that actually...

It's a little secret that in eras gone by, people understood. Many of the first nations peoples, indigenous Australians, native Americans still do. But the modern civilized world, you've forgotten.

Civilized!

(sigh)
That just means you live in towns – but you humans seem to think that it makes you somehow superior.

Now some of you, mainly new-agey folks and writers do understand alignment. Because it's not one of those secrets that has been kept hidden away; it's always been out there in plain sight but your so-called civilized humans have been conditioned to ignore it, and have screened it out.

Vincent

Come on, get to the point. Or if it's out there in plain sight, I'll Google it.

Roxy

Of course you can. Of course you can if want to.
You haven't touched your phone in five minutes. Do you have withdrawal symptoms?

Now listen up. You are born into this world in alignment. Got it? You are a spirit that has chosen to incarnate, to come into a physical body. That was a choice. Your choice. And while you were in the spirit world, you chose to have a particular experience in the physical that would align with the universe as it creates, expands and evolves. You can't do that from the spirit world. You have to get physical. In the spirit world, you know you are one with everything. You feel it. When you get physical, you become an individual and you lose that sense.

Vincent

(sings)

Let's get physical, physical.

Roxy

Nooooooooooooo. Enough!

Write me a new song sometime, same keywords, this new meaning.

The deal is that there can be no growth without challenge. To be sure, a balance of challenge and support; but there has to be challenge. It's Universal Law. And being physical would be totally pointless without growth. And so all you humans get challenges, starting from – or even before – birth. At some point, you'll have felt a lack of nurturing in some way from your mother. As children, you inherently feel the need for more nurturing than even the best mothers can provide. You felt a lack of acknowledgement from your father, a lack of appreciation for who you are and what you can achieve. As children, you inherently feel the need for more acknowledgement than even the best fathers can provide. It's just how it is. It's just how it has to be.

Because that happened in your childhood, you must find a way to cope and you do that through making up meaning about what's happening – what the lack of nurturing means about you. Perhaps you're not worthy. Perhaps you don't belong.

Whatever. You create a core belief that guides you through life and drives you to behave in ways that are totally dysfunctional.

> **Key insight:**
> We are born in alignment. Then, childhood wounding takes out out of alignment. We can choose to come back into alignment. However, even when we choose to align, life happens and it can move us out of alignment. Our aim is to continually come back into alignment.

So how do we get back into alignment?

Vincent

So how do we get back into alignment?

Roxy

Well, you've seen all those make more money ads on Facebook or Google. They'll help you get the home of your dreams, the car of your dreams, the getaways of your dreams, the partner of your dreams.

Vincent

Yes.

Roxy

What's wrong with that?

Vincent

You want me to be judgmental?

Roxy

No – just ask the right questions – so if there was something wrong with it what would it be?

Vincent

I don't know.

Roxy

Well at least you're honest. Human but honest.

Actually, you're not even honest because you do know; but I'll answer the question anyway,

What's wrong is that they tell you what your dreams are. But those aren't really your dreams. Thank God. I know what human dreams are really like. If they manifested, you'd be constantly chased by tigers, or be caught running naked through the shopping mall or God knows what else.

The home, the car, the getaways, the spouse – are they daydreams? Possibly.

But they're not even *your* daydreams.

They're visions of things that you've been told you should desire – and you've been told that since way back in childhood. They're just mirages.

No wonder you don't know what you really want from your life – you're so disconnected from it.

You humans need to start by getting off that couch.

I meant that metaphorically of course. I mean, Vincent, I know that, right now, you're sitting at your desk and typing up everything I say. And for the Flow Posse, it's once they've finished the book. I'm not expecting them to stand up and then carry on reading the next chapter.

Key insight:
You get back into alignment by simply choosing to. You can do this by shifting your state (3-4 deep breaths, holding at the end of both the inhale and exhale will help), tuning in to your intuition and taking whatever action it suggests.

How grandiose visions can keep you out of alignment

Now there is one final obstacle that gets in the way of you humans getting into alignment.

Vincent

And what's that?

Roxy

You ask what's my purpose in life? And expect a grandiose vision of a school in Africa or raising money for a hospital in India or something like that. Something quite grand. Something quite impressive.

Vincent

What's wrong with that? It sounds great to me.

Roxy

It's admirable. It's commendable. It's praiseworthy. It's true for some of you but not for all. What's it about? You humans are after the admiration and the recognition and the praise that comes from a big vision. And that stops you seeing your purpose when it calls out to you.

Vincent

So how do we know when our purpose is calling?

Roxy

That's easy. It comes from the heart. Consider that Mother Teresa started out, not by helping out hundreds of destitute women but just by opening her heart to just one. This happens with many people who you humans respect for living in line with their purpose. It can have very small beginnings. So what you humans need to do is to find what you love to do and stop worrying about the scale.

Come from your heart.

Stop trying to save the world or at least a big chunk of it and learn to respond from the heart.

Vincent

And is there a simple way to do that?

Roxy

Of course. And we will get to the practical work. For now, just understand that the vision of a grandiose purpose can often be out of alignment whenever that vision is about you and about how you look to others, not about what's coming from the heart.

Now. Alignment is a core idea. However, it's only the first that know about. The next one is structure. But before we go there, perhaps you'd like to summarize.

> **Key insight:**
> Alignment does not necessarily imply you have to have a grandiose vision to help all of humanity. You have to start by finding what you love to do and not worry about the scale.

Summary and next question.

Vincent

OK. Try this.

The universe will help you when you align with it, and with its creative expansive nature. We came into the world aligned, but were knocked out of alignment by our life experiences. And a major source of these experiences is our childhood wounding and our social conditioning.
So we end up wanting what we lack, rather than what we truly desire from our heart and soul.

And there is one other trap. We humans seem to have the idea that our purpose, our alignment needs to be grandiose and so because that's what we're looking for, we miss seeing the starting points right under our noses.

Roxy

Very good VG.

Vincent

So if having a beautiful aligned vision is a start, what do we need so that it's not just a beautiful daydream going nowhere?

Roxy

Aye, and you've had plenty of those haven't you. You could daydream your days away couldn't you.

But I'm not going to let you. Because to bring your vision into reality, you need structure; and that's next.

Chapter 10

What is structure and why is it so important?

What do you mean by structure

Vincent

What do you mean by structure?

Roxy

Great question. What would most humans say?

Vincent

Well, they'd probably think of a building.

Roxy

Perfect. And that's a physical structure.

What other sorts of structures do you have?

Vincent

Organizational structures?

Roxy

Very good, VG.

And do you remember from your corporate life how solid those structures were?

Vincent

> They were quite fluid. They'd change every twelve to eighteen months. Often for no apparent reason.

Roxy

> Oh, the reason is clear enough.
> Changing an organization's structure every so often makes it look like the management are working, even though it's mostly just an inessential distraction. You humans seem to think it's a lot easier than doing work that's actually productive ...
> What else has structure?

Vincent

> Music?

Roxy

> Of course. Complexity, delicacy, subtlety, rhythm, tonality or even atonality. Even heavy metal. It's that structure that separates it from pure noise.
>
> And?

Vincent

> Well, other art forms – visual arts, photography and video, prose and poetry.

Roxy

> Ah. Poetry
>
> I wandered lonely as a cloud...

Vincent

> Wordsworth

Roxy

> With me.
> It was such hard work.
>
> He was indolent, truth be told. Worked at a snail's pace.

(sigh)

And that's an insult to snails, seeing how quickly they ate all your parsley. You won't find that about him on Google, though.

I had to really nag him, poke and prod him and complain to him that day to get his backside out of his warm, cozy bed and go for that walk.

And I had to make sure he headed across the fields and not straight down to the local hostelry.

I wandered lonely as a cloud ...

Just him?
Never, I was there too every single step of the way.
The original was about BOTH of us, you know, but he wrote me out of it.
He told me his wife would never understand.

Vincent

I'm sorry Roxy, I didn't know.

Roxy

It didn't bother me. The poem got done.

So.

Buildings. Structures. So solid and physical.

Poetry – so structured, yet so ephemeral.

And yet there's a structure that's even more subtle.

It's structure in consciousness.

It holds the blueprint for a creation of the very multi-dimensionality of nature, of the universe.

> **Key insight:**
> There are many types of structures ranging from the physical like a building through a structure in an artistic creation through to the most subtle of all, a structure in consciousness. A structure is a combination of related parts that creates an end result.

Vincent

Seriously?

Roxy

You humans!

You just think of consciousness as a level of awareness.

For example, in a physical sense you see it as the awareness of your surroundings through your senses. If you get knocked unconscious, you have no awareness.

But you humans also have a more subtle meaning for consciousness too. For you, it's awareness that there are greater and more subtle forces at work in your lives and your energies. You have an awareness about the unseen. It's a subtle awareness and so you humans usually drown it out but you know you have it.

And then there is an even deeper meaning still.

Because consciousness is what creates the universe.

You've heard the quote "I think therefore I am". Descartes just didn't get it when I gave that to him.

(sigh)

My original was "I am conscious therefore I am", That's just a microcosm of what happens on a cosmic scale. Unfortunately, Descartes was part of the Age of Enlightenment and thinking was the fashion of the time. Humans! Why are you such faithful followers of fashion?

Vincent

I'm not.

Roxy

I can see that. And I don't just mean that your wardrobe needs an upgrade. It's about – or rather beyond – how you think and behave.

But, to return to consciousness ...

... consciousness is what shapes dimensions and laws, which shape both the physical and the non-physical. Consciousness created the structure in the universe that in turn gave all those big bang subatomic particles the blueprint to form gases and liquids and solids; rocks and minerals; and ultimately life.

Consciousness created the universe as creative, expanding and evolving; and in doing so, consciousness itself began to evolve until it could create advanced civilizations with beings who themselves create wonderful visions of the future.

Star Trek gave you humans the inkling that this was possible. At least, as far as they could, trying to capture the magnificence of advanced civilizations with the budget they had for set design in the 1960's.

Let's consider another example; a river. Water falls as rain on high ground.
Which way does it go?

Vincent

Down. Of course.

Roxy

Down? How does it go down?

Vincent

Well, some of it soaks into the land and some of it flows downhill over the land in streams, creeks, rivers; and eventually into the sea.

Roxy

So does the water say I'm up high and the shortest distance to the sea is in a particular direction so it makes most sense to flow directly that way? No, it just flows downwards because that's easiest. And because water will flow downhill only, the distance it travels to the sea can be many, many times the shortest most direct way. A great example is when the river meanders. The water in it flows downwards following the path of least resistance. Are you following me so far?

Vincent

Yes, that's pretty obvious.

Roxy

And that's my definition of structure. It's the universe evolving with the least amount of energy – or, better put, with the most efficient use of energy.

> **Key insight:**
> The universe evolves efficiently, using the least amount of energy necessary, and following the path of least resistance. It may appear to us to be slow, and meandering; but that is a powerful structure.

Vincent

I follow what you're saying but why is it so important for us to know that rivers flow downhill in curves and bends and meanders? Isn't that obvious?

A structure in consciousness is the path from where you are to where you want to be

Roxy

Humans! You never care to look beyond the superficial. Yes, it's obvious. But there's a deeper meaning that you're missing. You see your first question was indeed a good one.

Just as rivers flow downhill towards the sea, you have created a structure in consciousness that determines how you live in the physical – whether you've done that intentionally or unconsciously, by default. Humans also have the capacity to live with ease, using their energy super-efficiently to create amazing outcomes. Being aligned is the first part of it – it's like a choice to go downhill. And the structure is the path, the way from the beginning to the end, from where you are to where you want to be.

All you have to do to get what you want and what is in alignment for you is to create that structure intentionally, in your consciousness. You need a clear vision of your end result. And then you need to know exactly where you're at in the present. You need to know your starting point. The starting point and the end point create the structure.

> **Key insight:**
> A structure in consciousness comprises where you are at, where you want to be and the path between them that requires least energy.

And you know the consequences of getting the "where you're at right now" wrong?

Vincent

Yes. It's one of my favorite stories.

Roxy

So tell it.

Vincent

Well, it was in the British newspapers. A lady in the midlands wanted to give her partner a very special birthday present. He'd always wanted to go to Las Vegas. So she went online and found a really cheap deal from Birmingham airport and booked it. They rocked up to the airport but couldn't see their flight anywhere on the departures list. After a lot of panic and worry and dealing with helpful airport staff, the truth finally, finally dawned on them that the flights had been booked from Birmingham Alabama, not Birmingham, UK. Wrong starting point. They could have paid a lot more and got to Vegas but they ended up going to Amsterdam.

Now I'm not saying Amsterdam is better or worse than Vegas but it wasn't his dream destination.

Roxy

Exactly. They had the wrong starting point and so they did not get the outcome they were after.

When you have a true starting point and an end result that's in alignment, you have a creative structure.

Now there's one other important lesson here. Structures hold a tension and try to resolve that tension. If your structure is well constructed with a true starting point and an end result that's in alignment with your true potential, then the structure will resolve in favor of your end result. But if you have either wrong, the structure will resolve to give you a less-desirable outcome. Sometimes very undesirable.

> **Key insight:**
> A creative structure needs not only a true end result or vision but also a true starting point or current reality. If you are not clear and accurate about your starting point, the structure cannot resolve towards your end result and will instead resolve towards a less desirable outcome.

Creating dysfunctional structures

However, while you humans are capable of consciously creating structures that get you where you want to go, you can also unconsciously create structures that keep you well and truly stuck; and you humans are so, so creative, you can create even structures that oscillate!

How's your weight going?

Vincent

It's back up again today. I don't understand why. I haven't eaten much different from last week when it was coming off nicely, and I've actually done more exercise.

Oscillating structures

Roxy

Well, you do know weight loss is one of the most common oscillating structures you humans create. You set a target, go hard at it for a short while, results appear, and then you begin to go a little easier on yourselves. You give yourselves a wee treat. You cheat... just a little. And a little more each day until the weight starts going back up.

So you go back on the diet. You start losing weight. Then it's someone's birthday, you go to their party and some of that weight goes back on. You go back on the diet. You lose some weight. Then another celebration comes along – with feasting. And the weight goes back on.
And at first, an extra kilo or so is not too bad, it's not a concern until after a few days and a few extra kilos, it is and then it's back to the super-strict diet.

That's an oscillating structure – back and forth, up and down. And, Vincent, even you, with all your understanding of structures, have that one.

Vincent

Now you're making me feel bad. Embarrassed. I know I eat for comfort, but I find it very difficult to resist food, glorious food. I know it's not healthy and doesn't look good but it's hard.

Roxy

You want my help to control your eating?

Vincent

I don't believe you could.

Roxy

You are forgetting just how powerful I am. However, you can count yourself fortunate or, rather, unfortunate, that I am here to help you with this book, not to correct your eating habits.

That will come later, I promise you.

> **Key insight:**
> An oscillating structure moves backwards and forwards and never resolves to an end result. This is because it's a combination of two structures. One is taking you to your desired end result e.g., weight loss. The other, usually unconscious, is taking you to an opposing end result e.g., a desire for the pleasure that your diet has taken away.
>
> Because they never resolve to an end result, oscillating structures indicate that you are somehow sabotaging yourself.

Stuck structures

But we must move on, now, and talk about structures that are stuck. Give me an example.

Vincent

A mountain?

Roxy

Very good, VG. Mountains are indeed immoveable. Nearly. You humans have worked out how to blast them away for mining, or for transport tunnels or to run a freeway over the top, so stuck structures can be shifted, at least physical structures can, with enough effort and energy.

You can have stuck structures in consciousness too. It's when you have a vision you'd love but because of a deeply held belief or fear or definition, your unconscious will never allow yourself have it.

For example, you'd like to think you'd love to live in the country, in tranquility, beauty and proximity to nature. However, a part of you is so terrified of poisonous snakes or plagues of mice or wildfires; and that it holds you back from ever taking serious action towards creating it.

> **Key insight:**
> A stuck structure has no motion. If your structure in consciousness is stuck, it's because there is an equal and opposing force. Often, that's because you have a deeply held belief or fear (including the need for permission) that holds you back from moving forward.

So why would you humans create stuck or oscillating structures?
Structures that take you nowhere?

Vincent

I don't know. It doesn't make sense.

Roxy

Come on, don't play the fool, you do know.

Of course it doesn't make sense but you humans do it anyway. You always do.
You do it, Vincent. Just think of your weight. I know you rather

wouldn't. It's uncomfortable for you. But there you have an oscillating structure that you have created for yourself.

Why? You're a human. Why do you create these crazy structures that go nowhere?

And don't tell me you don't know because you do know but you just don't want to allow it into your awareness, let alone share it with me and the Flow Posse because that might be a wee bit uncomfortable for you.

Why do you create these crazy structures that go nowhere?

Vincent

We do it by default.
It's unconscious. We're not aware of it. But it has its roots in our responses to our childhood wounding, social conditioning and our traumas. We're usually oblivious to them. Often, we've suppressed them. We're very good at that.

Roxy

Too true. I've noticed.

So you have a vision or an end result, you make plans and start executing those plans but then you somehow manage to sabotage them. Why, Vincent? Why?

Vincent

I guess it's because we don't realize it's sabotage and so we call it bad luck or a mystifying loss of motivation or find some other explanation. But it's all that wounding and conditioning and trauma taking control and causing us to sabotage and the unwanted outcome.

Roxy

That's better. That's nearly a very good, VG.

I was beginning to doubt the wisdom of choosing to create this book with you.

I suppose you're just a little overawed at working with me.

And so you should be.
Just remember, I chose to work with you. You had no idea that you could even work with me. I think a little appreciation might be in order from time to time...

Vincent

Well you did choose to work with me and you are a pretty awesome muse so thanks – but don't get too smug. Just remember I can give you the flick and get another muse whenever I want so cut the control out.

Roxy

(laughs out loud)

Ah, another muse? Another sweet little junior like the one you started this book with?
You know that the book demanded that you work with me. You know that you didn't have the choice then, you don't now and you know the truth of that it in your heart.
So please, can I please have little bit less attitude, a little bit more gratitude, a little bit more humility and respect and a lot more nose to the grindstone.
And I say that with love. Tough love. We have this book to create.

Now where were we?
Yes, you humans do create dysfunctional structures in consciousness.

Choices

However, you can also create powerful creative structures in consciousness by consciously choosing your aligned end results.

And I use the word choosing with great care.

You don't hope or set intentions or plan because each of those has a way of weaseling out, like a get out clause. They inherently admit the possibility of not getting what you want...

And, tell me, Vincent, when you used to make plans at work, how did you build in you weasel exit?

Vincent

I didn't build weasel ways out into the plan.

Roxy

(laughs out loud)

Of course you didn't. You'd just wait till something happened to throw it off and then say, 'this was the plan but … '. But-head. Human businesses seem to accept but-heads. I guess it makes sense, otherwise they would never find anyone to employ.

You don't set goals either – goals are structures for the rational, mental, forcing way of working. At a deep level, the end purpose of any goal is to make yourself look good to others, whether it's your boss, your family, your friends, society. They're designed to shore up your identity; and in that they carry the seeds of sabotage. And so you humans often miss your goals.

You make choices from that place of alignment, the vision you have from your heart and soul. We'll give you the process soon enough. You choose what is true for you from all possible outcomes and focus on it like a laser beam until you have it. It's the way to get to your end results. This enables you to use your consciousness and the magic that flows from that, rather than rely solely on your logical mental processes which are always at risk of being undermined by the unconscious.

Vincent

Very good Roxy. You got that from one of the classes I ran, didn't you?

Roxy

Well, where do you think you got it from when you were preparing the class?

> **Key insight:**
> Choices from a place of inner authenticity establish the end result of a structure in consciousness. To complete the structure, we need to focus on the current reality i.e. where we're starting from right now – both physically and psychologically.

Summary and next question

So please now summarize this chapter.

Vincent

Well, all we need to do is create a choice that that is aligned with our hearts, our truth, and the universe; that has a defined end result – physical and emotional. Then we complete creating the structure in consciousness by acknowledging where we are now, the current reality. Then just as water flows down a river to the sea, the universe will be able to start helping us move to where we want to get to in the most efficient way – provided we do our part and stay in alignment.

Roxy

Very good, VG.

Vincent

And how can we be sure that the choice is aligned with the universe and our true potential?

Roxy

We'll cover that soon enough, Vincent.

For now, please recap, when a river flows to the sea, how hard does it have to work?

Vincent

It doesn't, it just flows.

Roxy

Very good VG.

The structure makes it happen. That is why structure is so important.

Vincent

So how do we go about creating structure?

Roxy

We'll come to that soon enough.

Next, we have to talk about energy.

Chapter 11

What is energy and why is it important?

Why is energy so important?

Vincent

> What do you mean? What about energy? Why is that so important?

Roxy

> What did your guide say when you went on that kayaking trip on the Yarra in March?

Vincent

> He said you're lucky. If you'd come yesterday, we would have cancelled the trip. There wasn't enough water in the river. But they've been letting some out of the dam.

Roxy

> And how was that trip?

Vincent

> Pretty awesome. Bright sunny day. Great guide. Fun rapids...

Roxy

> So it's not enough for the river to be naturally aligned to its end result and flow to the sea. It's not enough that it's carved out its bed to create the structure for the flow.
>
> It needs water to flow.

Tell me Vincent, did you try kayaking on the Todd River when you were in Alice Springs?

Structure on its own is not enough

Vincent

Are you kidding? Of course not. It was completely dried up. It usually is.

Although it did rain a couple of days after I left and then had water in it. There were videos on YouTube. Probably not good kayaking though, and probably no kayaks to be had there.

Roxy

And that's the point. It's not enough to make a fine and fancy choice that's aligned with the universe. It's not enough to create the structure by getting really real about where you're at right now.

If you don't put any energy in, your choice will be like the dried-up Todd River bed when you were standing in the middle of it taking selfies. Lots of potential but going nowhere.
The Todd River, that is, not you.

Figure 8: Vincent Standing in the middle of the Todd River, Alice Springs - 6 December 2020

Vincent

So how does that apply to us though creating our visions? How do the metaphors apply? What lessons are there in a dam that blocks the flow of a river? Or a river that only flows when there is a lot of rain?

Roxy

Well, those rivers that flow only when there's lots of rain, they're a metaphor for not putting energy in or just putting it in randomly for a day or two and then forgetting about it.

It's a metaphor for reading or repeating the words of the visions and outcomes you want but not really feeling it, not having your heart in it, not embodying how you feel in that end result.

It's a metaphor for failing to take action when what needs to be done is obvious, when the action is crying out to be taken. It's as if you deliberately look the other way when action is required. It's when you hope your choice doesn't demand action.

You just shut it all down before it can demand that you actually do anything.

That's how to keep the energy out your of choices. It's like there was never any energy there in the first place. Just like there wasn't water in the Todd River.

> **Key insight:**
> Having the right structure is not enough. For the end results to be created, you have to put energy in.

Vincent

Why would anybody do that? Waste all that energy creating choices and then stop?

Roxy

Because you're just humans. That's just how you are.
Look, Vincent, you know these people. It drives you crazy. They drive you crazy. It's as if you give them a 3D printer that will print anything they want and they look at it, admire it, and all they do is post pictures of it on social media.

But they actually never hook it up and make anything with it. It infuriates you, doesn't it?

Especially when those of your coaching clients that do actually make a habit of putting in the energy get themselves into the flow end up receiving magical synchronicities and coincidences and opportunities.

Vincent

Not much infuriates me but that does. For sure.

Why do humans build dams?

Roxy

So tell me about the dams. Why do you build dams?

Vincent

To supply water to the towns and cities.

Roxy

Vincent, you think you're so clever.

Just one answer? Come on. Get creative!

Why do you humans build dams?

Vincent

Also to generate hydroelectric power.

Roxy

Good... And?

Vincent

And to control floods.

Roxy

And?

Vincent

Holding back pollutants like at mines

Roxy

Now you're getting creative. Now you have a flow of ideas. And?

Vincent

And there are still all those mill ponds around England that used to power water mills.

Roxy

And?

Vincent

And beavers build dams to protect their lodges.

Roxy

Good. Very perceptive. It's not just humans who build dams.

Vincent

Oh, and to control the flow of a river so boats can navigate it more easily.

Roxy

Very good, VG.

So you would have to agree that dams are extremely useful creations then.

Vincent

That's an understatement.

So what's not to like about dams?

Roxy

So what could possibly be wrong with dams?

Vincent

What do you mean?

Roxy

Oh Vincent, you've switched your brain off again.

And I say that with love. Tough love.

Come on. You were flowing the answers out a couple of minutes ago.

> I was asking you what could possibly be wrong with dams? What downsides are there? There must be some. Get creative.

Vincent

Well sometimes one group of people and one ecosystem benefits because they get the water; but it's at the expense of others. A dam built to create a reservoir for drinking water holds up water from lower down in the river and that's not good for the fish and the platypuses and the river life. Or for kayakers.

Roxy

That's a start. And?

Vincent

And some rivers like the Tigris and the Euphrates that flow across multiple countries. And the ones upstream want to dam it and leave less water for the ones downstream.

Roxy

And?

Vincent

People used to depend on the Nile flooding in Egypt to irrigate and fertilize their land and that all stopped with the Aswan dam.

Roxy

And?

Vincent

Some dams hold meltwater from the spring thaws instead of letting it flow downriver. So the water stays cold. And then when it's released in the summer, it's much colder than it was before the dam was built and it wrecks the ecosystems.

Roxy

And?

Vincent

    Some species need to migrate up and down rivers to and from breeding grounds; and dams stop that.

Roxy

    And?

Vincent

    OMG how much more do you want?

Roxy

    You were flowing so well. And you said you were working with me. Then when I make you do some actual work you complain?

    Why? Why?

    (Big sigh)

    Humans!

What do dams show us about energy?

So, just like a dam, a similar dynamic occurs with choices. You humans are extremely capable of generating a lot of energy. It's just that you need to release it in a powerful, controlled way so that it helps create the results you're after.

> **Key insight:**
> We need to infuse a structure with a consistent flow of energy in order to get the end results that we choose.

Sprinters

Some of you humans start out very frustrated. Some of you are even angry. You want everything now. So you let all that energy go at once.

There's a flurry of action, perhaps a leap forward, perhaps a lot of effort expended on action that goes nowhere. You get beautiful business cards, create a gorgeous-looking website, make a handful of delightful posts on social media. And then you run out of energy. Everything goes to pot and grinds to a halt without creating any meaningful results.

You've been there haven't you?

Vincent

Possibly ...

Roxy

Oh, come on Vincent, how many boxes of your old business cards do you have?

The structure you create requires energy to be managed like a marathon and, when you're frustrated or angry, you manage the energy like a sprint. You don't get very far that way do you?

And then you see what underlies all this anger and frustration – it's powerlessness. You're out of energy. Have you been there?

Vincent

Yes. In deep.

> **Key insight:**
> Some humans jump into a new project full of energy but then dissipate it all, quickly. Structures need a consistent flow of energy for the end result to be created.

The debilitating nature of fear

Roxy

Other times, you don't let any energy go at all... Why not?

And, Vincent, don't answer that. I will for once...

It's fear. See, letting energy flow into your choice means taking action. Often it means putting yourself on the line. It means standing up for your message in public. It means being seen. And you humans find that scary.

You know what the number one fear humans have is?

Vincent

The mobile phone battery going flat?

Roxy

Seriously?

Vincent

With no way to charge it?

Roxy

Vincent!

(pause)

I'm so sorry. You're absolutely right. I'm a wee bit behind the times.

So what's the number two fear humans have which, until the start of the 21st century, was the number one fear?

Vincent

Ah. Public speaking?

Roxy

Now there speaks someone who's been in Toastmasters.

It conveniently ignores the folks in places like India – their fear is whether there's a meal today.

But getting really vulnerable in public, whether it's speaking or writing or even just conversing with a loved one with different points of view, that does put the fear of God into most of you humans.

Although it had to be a human who created this idea of God as a male figure who had to be feared. Humans! How ridiculous! All those pastors, preachers and priests have no idea.

God is so much closer to that image of love and support we see on the Sistine Chapel ceiling.

Vincent

Really?

Roxy

You humans don't have the language or the senses to even begin to comprehend God, even though your souls are created as hologram-perfect images.

(big sigh)

Fear of vulnerability

Now, where were we? Even though your souls are hologram-perfect images of God, you humans fear vulnerability.

You fear the consequences of being vulnerable, of being judged, being rejected, of not belonging, of being found out as worthless, as an imposter. And all that holds up the energy like a dam holds up water. And do you know what you humans say?

Vincent

Go on. Tell me. We talk a lot of BS that we don't mean.

Roxy

Aye. I've been working with humans for millennia; and I found that out on the very first day.

But you humans are also on the right track when you say you can smell the fear.

It's a common way you humans connect with intuition without knowing it. You smell the fear in others. And fear is something your so-called deodorants amplify, not eliminate. Although, I have to say, there's not a lot of fear around to be smelled because you humans are so fearful of the feeling the fear[3] that you've made the job of modifying your behavior so that you avoid it altogether into an art form.

That's a subject for a whole other book you're going to be writing with me; Which will be another one of the series we're creating together. Don't get your hopes up that you're done with me after this one. I know that's your biggest fear because you think I make you work hard… But I digress…

Certainly, fear holds up the energy.

> **Key insight:**
> Fear restricts or even completely blocks our ability to put energy into a structure.

Depression does too.

Depression

Vincent

Well, that's hardly a surprise.

Roxy

Many of you humans have serious mental health issues, and are clinically depressed. This work is not for them for now. They need professional help first.

But many, many more of you humans have what appears to be a mild form of depression. That quiet desperation Thoreau wrote about. You lack energy. You're listless and lethargic. You hold an unconscious belief that nothing you do will be

---

3 Roxy says,
 The quote you now know as "There is nothing to fear but fear itself" originated with Michel de Montaigne in 16th century France. He was brilliant to work with. We invented the essay together. School students across the world now curse him for that. You have to be thick-skinned to work with a great muse like me.

of any use, nor of any consequence. Most of the time, that's underpinned by a belief that you're not worthy or not good enough or just don't belong. It makes life feel kind of pointless.

Do you know people like that?

Vincent

Tons of them.

> **Key insight:**
> Unconscious beliefs can stop us putting ANY energy in and making progress or even getting started on the journey to our end results.

Summary

Roxy

You see?

You humans could create so much more if you understood what was holding you back.

But at least it's good that you recognize it in yourself and others.

So please summarize.

Vincent

Structure without energy has no flow. Like the Todd River. Remember my selfie?

You need a steady flow of energy in your lives. Not a flow that's dammed up and never released because of fear or other feelings, beliefs or assumptions; the fear of vulnerability; and the fear of fear itself. Not a flow that like a burst dam – all there one minute and gone the next.

Roxy

Very good, VG.

Vincent

So now we know what alignment and structure and energy are, how do we go about creating and using them?

Roxy

Well, first you need a few basics. That's what we'll address next.

Part 4

Intuitive skills and tools for getting into the flow

Chapter 12

Introduction to the skills and tools

Roxy

> Who are you?

Vincent

> I'm Vincent and why are you asking me dumb questions? Again?

Roxy

> Humans! I ask a profound metaphysical question, probably the most profound metaphysical question there is; and all I get is attitude. Tell me, who is Vincent?

Vincent

> Oh. You want the deep metaphysical answer?

Roxy

> I most certainly don't want the dumb one again...

Vincent

> The one that's beyond words?

Roxy

> Yes. But I need you to try and find some words anyway.

Vincent

> Well, I guess the true, essential part of me is marvelous, magnificent and magical beyond my normal comprehension. Powerful too.

Roxy

You guess? You're just guessing?

Vincent

Actually no, I know. At a profound level, I know.

Roxy

That's better.

So when you introduce yourself socially, how do you do it? Once you've got past exchanging names, of course.

Vincent

It depends on the group and its interests. I could talk about my kids and family. I often talk about my work.

Roxy

That's exactly how you humans think and behave – because you define yourselves by roles you play-out and the labels you place on yourselves. Parent. Worker. Perhaps a hobby, an interest, or, too often, an affliction.

Vincent

An affliction? Like Blind Lemon Jefferson?

Roxy

Asthmatic Vincent Melling doesn't have the same ring does it?

Yet you so-called modern humans have created a plethora of new labels of affliction although none as physically challenging as those blues singers.

So who are you, Vincent, beyond the labels?

Vincent

You guys in the spirit world keep telling us we're a combination of aspects. Our true essence is a multidimensional infinite powerful loving soul that lives forever. Some say through many lifetimes. But there's also the physical part – our bodies.

Roxy

Yes, you are all souls with physical bodies. And with your physicality comes your psychological makeup, your personality. All humans have a personality; yes, even accountants.

Your personalities are created in childhood in response to the challenges and traumas there and include all those unconscious beliefs, fears, definitions and assumptions. What most of you don't realize is that, by default it runs your lives. Your unconscious gives rise to a plethora of feelings, emotions, and thoughts, which just aren't real.[1] They're just like an old but familiar and somehow comforting soundtrack to your life.

Now the soul part of you knows where it wants to go. But in most of you, it's that dysfunctional soundtrack that drives your behavior and what you actually create. And the sad thing is that most of you don't see it for what it is. You believe it's real. So you never get to know your soul and what it wants.

Vincent

And the core tools of intuition are about doing that?

Roxy

Exactly. There are four parts to the work.
First, you have to reconnect with your intuition and learn what it looks and feels like and how different the world appears when you are connected.
Next, you need to learn how to get information you can use on demand.
Then you can use that intuitive connection to find out exactly what your soul wants. We've called that alignment.
Finally, you have to get to know your unconscious, your shadow. You have to familiarize yourself with its tricks and triggers. Get ahead of its game. Then you can start to move forward on your path of greatness.

---

[1] Vincent says this is described very well in

Hawkins, David R. *Letting Go: The Pathway of Surrender* (Chapter 3 - The Anatomy Of Emotions) Veritas Publishing.

> **Key insight:**
> There are four stages to working with intuition.
>
> 1. Reconnect with your intuition.
>
> 2. Learn how you can get information you can use - on demand.
>
> 3. Use that intuitive connection to find your alignment; what's true for you to choose in your life.
>
> 4. Get to know your unconscious / shadow / sabotage and how to stay one step ahead.

Chapter 13

Meet your intuition with the Innosence² exercise

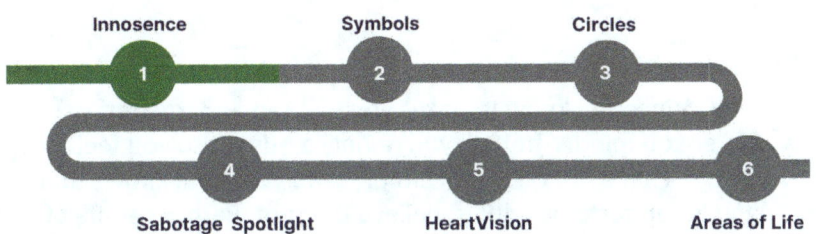

Get it done

Roxy

Let's start with the first tool – the innosence exercise. Now I know some of our Flow Posse are going to say, 'Does this have a guided meditation? About time, I love them'.

Vincent

Yes. And they'll work with it for a couple of goes and then lose interest. How do we deal with that?

---

2 Vincent writes - Innosense is spelled this way as a concatenation of "in no sense". This is because the innosense meditation takes us out of the place where our limiting beliefs, assumptions and definitions could cause us to judge the information we get (and where we'd tell ourselves, 'this makes no sense') and into a non-judgemental state where we're opened up to receive information from our intuition.

Roxy

Humans!

We just write the book, Vincent. We can't make them do it. That's not our work – or at least it's not the work of the book.

Vincent

And what about the others who say, 'oh no, not an exercise where I have to stop reading and do something' and they won't even give it a go. I sometimes feel we're wasting our time with this.

Roxy

Look, Vincent, I know it makes you feel sad and frustrated, but never you mind. After all, you're only a human so you feel these things. That's not our work either – and your soul knows that and is comfortable with it, believe it or not. Perhaps some of them will come back to it at some point and do it because it is truly transformational. Perhaps not. We can but offer it.

Humans!

But be encouraged because many of you in our Flow Posse will take this exercise and use it. And like with any state-changing meditation, you can anchor the end state and so get back to that state of innosense very, very quickly – in a few seconds. How long does it take you, Vincent?

Vincent

You're right. The first time I came to the state of innosense was through the exercise. For the second time, the facilitator said we could get there quickly and, as it turned out, I could. In a few seconds. And it's been the same ever since.

Why we do the innosense exercise

Roxy

Very good, VG.

Now there is a reason why we teach this particular exercise. It starts with a meditation that has been specifically created to take you to a place where your unconscious is inactivated. Switched off. It takes you back to a place before it was even formed. That soundtrack of thoughts and feelings is paused. From this place, everything you receive comes from your intuition, from your soul. There's nowhere else for it to come from. This is why it's called in-no-sense because you have silenced those thoughts and feelings.

> **Key insight:**
>
> **Why we do the innosense meditation?**
> Reason # 1
> It shuts down our unconscious minds and interrupts our background soundtrack of thoughts, feelings and emotions; and it opens us up to our intuition and to seeing the world differently.

Opening up to receive more information

There's another incredibly useful and important aspect of the innosense meditation. You see, you humans filter everything you perceive. You have invented language.
Now that is essential for communication but it has a downside that you don't often consider. You look at a tree and say that's a tree; but you're not really seeing the tree. In fact, you're reducing the tree to a label when you could sense it in so many ways, and some of those ways are exquisitely subtle. From your mind's point of view, it's wonderful that you've identified and labelled the tree as a tree and now it's freed up to move on to the next thing. What the innosense meditation does is quieten the mind to the point where it fully senses the tree. The complexity in the bark. In the leaves, the flowers, the fruits or nuts. The tiny ants crawling up it and the bird perching in its branches. The energy it holds and emanates.

What's going on for you as I say this?

Vincent

I'm picturing everything you say. What have I done wrong now?

Roxy

Oh the guilt, oh the fear.

Humans!

This time you've done nothing wrong. This time, you have a perfect answer.

But you can be sure that as many of our Flow Posse read this, their minds are in control. The thing we have labelled as a tree now has a number of labels of its various component parts – bark, leave, flower, but they are still all labels and the wonder of creation that you were picturing passes them by. And the meditation will help them get past that.

There are other parts of the mind that filter information. The reptilian brain has the job of filtering what you need to survive from everything else. It evolved to keep you safe from predators like sabre tooth tigers, lions, and wolves. I was going to add lawyers but one of them would sue you if I did. If what is perceived is not dangerous or new or different the reptilian brain filters it out.

Dr. Andrew B Newberg has said, 'Our brain receives 400 billion bits/second of information, but we're only aware of 2000 bits/second. Reality is happening in our brain all the time – we're receiving it but it's not being integrated.'[3]

Your mind gets so focused, it's simply not aware of everything that's available to it consciously, let alone what it can pick up through intuition. And the innosense meditation removes that 2000 bits/second filter and opens you up to receive the information that's available and important for you.

---

3   This quote is from Andrew B Newberg, (MD, Radiologist), in the movie 'What the Bleep Do We Know?'

> **Key insight:**
> Why we do the innosense meditation?
> Reason # 2
> It removes the filters on our everyday perception that limit the data that we receive so that we're open to all the information that's available and important to us.

Finding the right space

You could do this exercise anytime, anywhere. But you won't really get the best experience unless you can get the right space.

Vincent

So what does that look like?

Roxy

Why are you asking me? You know. You've done it so often. You could do it in your sleep. Maybe you do. I don't stay around after our writing sessions. So you do some of the work for a change. You tell the Flow Posse.

Humans!

Vincent

I can never get it right for you, can I?

Roxy

Never say never again. I just said you gave me a perfect answer to my last question. I just told you how perfectly qualified you are to do it. And that hasn't stopped you from regressing all the way back into your shell.

Humans!

Just get over yourself, Vincent, and get on with it.

And I say that with love. Tough love.

Guidelines and directions for the innosense exercise

Vincent

The meditation is available online and the link is at the end of the guidelines for getting into the right space.

Number one – be safe. Don't listen to the meditation while you're driving or operating machinery. Same as any other meditation. You just need a quiet place to sit and be still.

Number two – be sober, like any meditation. It needs to be said.

Number three – Make sure you have an hour to do it – allow thirty minutes after the meditation to go for a walk and a further fifteen minutes to journal or record your experience.

Roxy

Very good, VG. I just want to emphasize that this is an exercise. The meditation is just the first part of the exercise. You don't stop there. Carry on, Vincent.

Vincent

Number four – ideally, do it in daylight. It will work much better for you.

Number five – ideally, do it in nature. If you have a back yard, great. Or perhaps you live close to a park, a creek, a river or a beach where you can walk. Or perhaps drive to a park, park your car, and then listen to the meditation.

Roxy

Remember, don't listen while you're driving. I'm sorry, I have to repeat that, but there are some incredibly dumb humans out there.
Some?
Plenty.

(sigh)

I'm sorry, Vincent, I interrupted you. Had you finished?

Vincent

No. Still a couple to go.

Number six – at the end of the meditation, you'll be invited take a walk and really observe anything that catches your eye. The best experiences will come from nature. Leaves, flowers, birds, butterflies, a river, whatever you have access to. You can also observe a few man-made items as well to compare the experience.

Number seven – Record your impressions or journal them. Allow some time for this. Ask yourself what did I experience? Then answer the questions; what did I feel? What did I learn?

How was that, Roxy?

Roxy

Very good, Vincent.

Anchoring innosense

Here's how the Flow Posse can get to really anchor the experience.

When you've completed the journaling, take a break. Do something mental that will take you out of the state. Watch a video. Play a game.

THEN

Practice going back into innosense without doing the full meditation. Just close your eyes, focus on your breath, relax the body, drop a little deeper and then set the intention to go into innosense. And then go there and know that the higher part of you has already learned exactly how to do it. Check by observing the trees or plants or a pot plant, anything natural if you can.

And repeat. Go back to the mental state and then drop back into innosense until you're confident you can just get present, set the intention and go straight there very quickly. It should only take a very few cycles to really anchor it.

The Innosense exercise

> **Resources**
> Here's the link to the meditation that Vincent has very thoughtfully recorded for you.
>
> https://vincentgmelling.com/gitf-in-no-sense
>
> There is also a recap of the guidelines and key steps to the meditation in Appendix 1 Exercises and resources in case, for any reason, you can't access the audio

Vincent

    Thanks Roxy. What's next?

Roxy

    Ideally, our Flow Posse should stop here and do the exercise. If it was an in-person or online training, you would take them through it.

    But no. This is a book. You can guarantee most of them will keep reading. It may be night. They may not have a full hour right now. They may be mid-commute and reading on the train or listening to the audio version like you used to do. So, Flow Posse, if you're not in an ideal place at an ideal time, please, please commit to coming back to it, OK? This is foundational. Promise me.

And to make it easier for you, Vincent has created a consolidated list of the links to all the exercises in Appendix 1

Exercises and resources

Now, I'm going to create some suspense ...

When and only when you've done the exercise, and not before, if you want to compare notes, take a look at ... Appendix 2

Vincent's experience with the innosense meditation.

Vincent, it's time for one of your wonderful summaries, and I say that with love and not tough love. At least, not this time.

Summary

Vincent

In this chapter, we met the innosense meditation. It's a powerful way to connect with your intuition. It takes you to a place where you're free from the thoughts and feelings that come from your unconscious shadow; a place where you're open to receive from intuition; and a place where you observe and receive infinitely more information and detail than your normal conscious state allows because the filters on your everyday perception have dropped away, as has your mind's tendency to label everything.

This was the first part of an exercise that shows you how different things look when you're in the state of innosense; and then gave you guidelines to anchor that state.

Roxy

That's perfect.

Vincent

So now we can get into this powerful intuitive state, how can we use it to get helpful information?

Roxy
    That's up next.

Chapter 14

Symbols

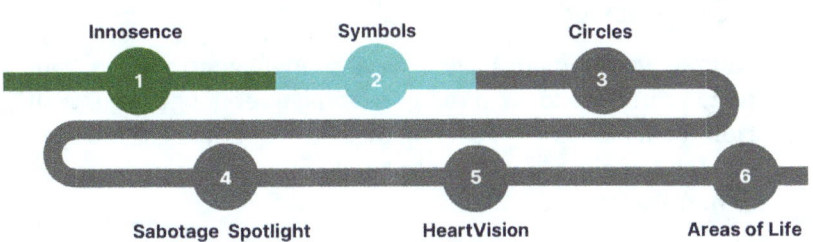

The language of intuition

Roxy

Welcome to today's session, Vincent.

So please remind me, what language are we speaking in today?

Vincent

Klingon? Elvish? Esperanto? Apparently not, Español hoy?

What does it sound like?

Roxy

It's not a stupid question so I do not expect a stupid answer.

But I guess you're a human so it's always a possibility; or, should I say, a likelihood.

No, no, no! It's a simple question. I am looking for a simple answer.
Which, apparently, is somewhat challenging for you today.

There are no hidden agendas. I promise you.

What language are we working in?

Vincent

English. The language of Shakespeare, of Wordsworth of…

Roxy

OK, Vincent, OK. We don't have time to list every single author I've ever worked with.

You see, you humans have to have a language to survive. You need to be able to label things that might endanger you. Wolf! Lion! Bear! Electricity! Car! All these things could kill you or your children and you need to be able to warn them to get out of harm's way.

And then you need language to function in the world. Do you remember that story about Helen Keller?

> **Key insight:**
> We all need a language to function in the world.

Vincent

Sort of – could you remind me?

Roxy

No. Research is your job. Go off and do it …

Vincent

… As a young child, she had barely learned language as she lacked the ability to hear, to see, or to speak. What little language she had was a result of her communicating with her teacher by spelling words by touching each other's hand. The world was very confusing for her as she had so little vocabulary, yet so much to communicate to cover even the basics of living. Then one day, she was holding a mug under the water pump.

The cold water spilled over her hand, the sensation shocked her and something shifted for her. At that point, she started to ask the names of all the objects in her world. Her existence without language was confusing and frustrating. And after this experience, as she expanded her vocabulary, she became happier and joyful.

Roxy

Exactly. You humans need language to communicate with each other – at least until you finally develop your telepathic abilities.

Are you up for writing a book about that?

Vincent

As you're so staggeringly telepathic, don't you know the answer already?

Roxy

Of course I do. You are not up for writing that book. But the Flow Posse needs to know that, and it would have been wise of you to just answer the question.

Now, I'm sorry but I have no choice, I'm going to have to tell everyone what excuses you have for not writing that book. You're feeling resistance, overwhelm, tired, not to mention, and I've said this before, you appear to be allergic to hard work.

Vincent

I'm not...

Roxy

And I know what you're thinking – as so you rightly said, I am telepathic. So, no, I am not "a dominating slave driver". I give you love. Lots of love. Tough love.

So, of course, your excuses are just excuses. We'll go into that more in the chapter on the shadow.
After all, what could be cooler than a book on telepathy? We

will revisit that sometime in the future. I won't forget. I have a phenomenal memory and we don't get Alzheimer's in the spirit world.

How does intuition communicate?

So, Vincent, I'm going to have to ask you do some more work. Please would you compare language with intuition. Does intuition communicate with you in clear labels and carefully constructed sentences? In concise couplets or flowing iambic pentameter?

Vincent

No. Sometimes intuition gives me a word or a short phrase but often it's visual or just a subtle feeling.

Roxy

Exactly. Intuition can come to you in a number of ways. And it shows up differently for everybody. Some of you will get a vision, sometimes you hear it, a conversation or just a word or a phrase, and sometimes you just feel it. That's tough to get over for you humans – you have been so conditioned to the idea that intuition shows up the same for everybody, every time. You expect Technicolor visuals. You expect guides conversing at length with you. That's how it is for a few of you. But for most it's more subtle. But just as powerful.

> **Key insight:**
> The language of intuition is symbols. Often symbols are visual but they can also be words, a sound, or a feeling.

Why symbols?

However, one of most powerful ways intuition communicates is with symbols and they are usually visual. Do you know why?

Vincent

Of course I do.

(pause with an air of finality)

Roxy

(disdainful sigh)

It's a reasonable request. So are you going to grace us with the answer or are you just going to play stupid?

Vincent

Well, we humans say a picture is worth 1000 words ...

Roxy

That's better. Exactly. And that begins to explain why the language of intuition is symbols. A symbol can be rich in detail and carry profound meaning.

So how do you interpret them? You have to use your imagination.

With the combination of the visual content and what you contribute through imagination, a symbol can communicate vast amounts of information in a deceptively simple form.

That's why symbols are the language of intuition.

> **Key insight:**
> Symbols are often rich in detail and carry a profound meaning

What's a symbol?

Now tell our Flow Posse what a symbol is.

Vincent

>A symbol is a visual image. It may be very clear. A bird, a candlestick, even a whole scene. Or it may be abstract – just a line or a flash of lightning. Or even blank.
>
>It can be still or in motion.

What do symbols mean?

Roxy

>Very good, VG. So how do you unpack what your symbols mean?

Vincent

>Intuition will tell you what they mean and it's not the same every time.
>
>You might see a brightly colored parrot flying swiftly through the air from tree to tree on a bright sunny day. Another time, you might see a similar parrot but the plumage is somehow duller, it's pouring with rain, it flies a shorter distance.

Roxy

>Very good. Now there are some humans who'd look up their 'Junior dictionary of symbols in dreams and visions' and find 'parrot meaning in vision/dreams'. Perhaps they'd read that it means "to mindlessly repeat whatever it hears".
>
>And some of you humans teach your parrots the most vulgar profanities and abuse.
>Do you know anybody like that?

Vincent

>Not personally. But apparently the Lincolnshire Wildlife Park in England had to move on five African Grey parrots for swearing at each other.

Roxy

Humans!

I know you find that amusing, Vincent, but I was not asking about swearing parrots. I clearly wasn't clear enough for you. And I wasn't asking about humans who mindlessly repeat whatever nonsense they hear either.

I was asking whether you know anybody that who look up symbolic meanings in a reference book?

Vincent

A few.

Roxy

But that's not how to get powerful information from a symbol.

Would one who parrots what they read in a book be a valid interpretation for both of those parrot visions you described?

Vincent

Obviously not. What's obvious is that the first vision is talking about a bright positive active energy, while the second talks to a duller, less inspiring energy. Obviously, there'd be far more to the reading than that. That's just the starting point.

Looking for detail in a symbol

Roxy

Of course. You will be fed by your intuition as you continue to interpret the symbol.

Vincent

But you can also go back to the symbol, the vision and look for detail to interpret. What color is the parrot's plumage? Its breast?
What's in the background? On a sunny day where in the sky is the sun? And what does that tell you about the season and

time of day? Is there anything significant about the foliage, fruits, nuts, or seeds, or any flowers on the tree? What does that suggest about the location? There's tons of detail in the vision that you can interpret.

The importance of meaning.

Roxy

> That's a lot of detail you can get out of the vision. But what does it all mean?

Vincent

> That's where the rubber hits the road. I remember being read in one group and the person reading me said that when they tuned in, they got an owl.

Roxy

> And what did they say that meant?

Vincent

> They just sat back with a smug smile. No interpretation offered. So their reading had told me nothing about myself and nothing that was useful to me.
>
> That's pointless. You have to interpret the information you're receiving from the symbol and ask yourself what does it all mean?

> **Key insight:**
> Intuition will inform you about what the obvious meaning of the symbol it. Similar symbols can have different meanings, for example, if there are differences in the mood, the background or the energy of the image.

Using imagination.

That answer will also come intuitively and be related to the intention that you tune in with. The answer may come as what's intuitively obvious or you may need to use your imagination and make it up.

Roxy

Imagination eh?

Don't you humans tell your kids, 'you're just imagining it' as if imagination is something you really have to keep under control?

Don't you say that this person has a vivid imagination in a very disparaging, sarcastic tone of voice?

Don't you humans treat imagination as daydreaming, disassociation, escaping from or avoiding reality?

Am I right? Or am I right?

Vincent

That's exactly how many of us treat imagination.

Roxy

And here is what the consequence of that is.

When you disparage imagination, it's your shadow talking. Because it knows that using your imagination has the potential to break out of the psychological safety zone it's trying to keep you in and take you into your higher creative nature.

Imagination is the faculty that conceives of and sees all sorts of structures – artworks, buildings, processes, businesses BEFORE they have been created and leads you towards creating them. Imagination is the faculty of creating the idea of new things in consciousness so they can be brought into physical being.

Vincent

But we do praise our kids for the art they bring home from school, for something they've written for being imaginative.

Roxy

> True. For most of you humans, imagination is good as long as it stays in its box. You'll guide your children to imagine their future and tell them that the world is their oyster; then, years later, react with disbelief, disappointment and resentment when the young adult children announce that they're moving overseas.
>
> The minute imagination threatens to escape from the box, you see it as dangerous. You even talk about an over-active imagination like it's a bad thing.
>
> But imagination is more than a powerful creative force. It's also part of your system for receiving intuition. You've been told that when you have run out of insights, vision, energy to interpret, you just make it up based on what's obvious. And that's the point. Being in the energy of what's obvious feeds you with the information through your imagination. It feels like you're making it up but you're actually pulling intuitive information from a very subtle place.
>
> And you humans try and stifle it from the youngest age.

Vincent

> Wow, that's awesome – I've never heard it put like that before.

Roxy

> Well I don't like to blow my own trumpet but...

Vincent

> Yes you do. All the bloody time.
>
> I wrote Shakespeare. I wrote Wordsworth. I'm a powerful cosmic multidimensional mega-being.
>
> Come on!

Roxy

> Humans!

> That's just the plain truth. No more, no less. Do you have a problem accepting that?

Vincent

> No but...

> **Key insight:**
> Imagination is a powerful aspect of intuition. If you hold yourself in the vibration of your intuition space and you make up the meaning of a symbol based on what's most intuitively obvious, it will have a ring of truth to it. You'll surprise yourself at how accurate you are with making it up.

Summary

Roxy

> Not buts, but-head.
>
> Please summarize symbols so we can move on.

Vincent

> OK, if you promise not to call me a but-head anymore.

Roxy

> I can't promise the anymore part. Because you humans are all such but-heads that it's like you continually keep reminding me to call you a but-head.
>
> But I'll do my best.

Vincent

> And I'll be listening and watching.
>
> Symbols are a powerful intuitive tool that give us a vast amount of complex information through a deceptively simple form – usually through an image. You need to interpret your symbol,

not by looking it up in a book, but by using your intuition to get the full message. And there is a ton of detail in a symbol that can give up information. And when you run out of that material, you just use your imagination to interpret what else is obvious.

Roxy

Finally. Very good, VG.

Now we can move on to another powerful intuitive tool. Circles.

Chapter 15

Circles

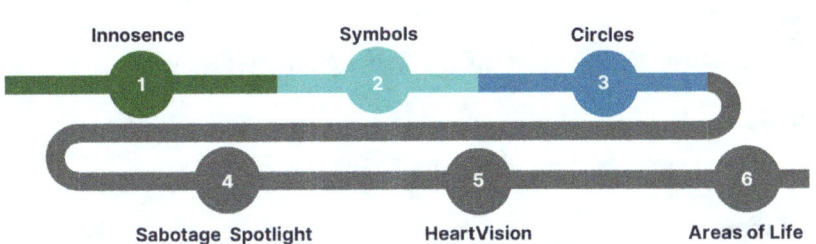

Why circles?

Roxy
> Vincent, when a drop of water falls on a surface, for example, a kitchen bench, what shape does it form?

Vincent
> It's round.

Roxy
> Vincent! Round is not the name of a geometric shape and well you know it.
> What shape does it form?

Vincent
> A circle? No, actually, a hemisphere?

Roxy
> So, tell me., why would that be?

Vincent

Surface tension.

Roxy

Typical human. You give me a label. Two words. You don't look deeper.

It's a miracle that it forms a circle so why does it form a circle?

Vincent

Because it's the most efficient shape energetically?

Roxy

Now you're getting somewhere. Tell me more.

Vincent

But I'd have to look up the physics of surface tension online.

Roxy

You can't wait to get your hands on your phone again.
I can tell.
Just use your imagination, Vincent.

Vincent

OK. Because a spherical drop results in the least surface area for the volume of that drop.

Roxy

That's a good start. What else?

Vincent

Circular shapes are stronger than angular shapes – which have weaknesses at the corners.

Roxy

Very good. Very good. So circles are strong energetic shapes.

Imagine a time thousands of years ago. It's a winter's evening.

Villagers are gathered around a big fire. What shape do they form?

Vincent

A circle. So everyone is equidistant from the fire, sharing its warmth.

Roxy

And, so circles have the energy of coming together don't they?

There are many examples of circles in nature. But humans also created circles – like Stonehenge and all those other stone circles in England. Why?

Vincent

They were like astronomical computers. The alignment of the stones helped the people of the time determine solstices and many other significant astronomical events.

Roxy

So why was Stonehenge round? Your 21st century computers are pretty much oblong aren't they?

Vincent

I guess Stonehenge had to be round because the sun, moon and stars also move in circles. Would that be why?

Roxy

Well, your solar system is certainly full of motion that is pretty much circular – planets around the sun, moons around the planets. The asteroid belt.

Vincent

So why are you asking me all these questions about circles?

Roxy

It's my job.

Vincent

It's nice to think you're actually doing some work.

But it's a kind of a catch 22 for me. If you work I have to work even harder.

Roxy

And?

I have better things to do with our time than continually repeat myself about how hard it is to extract useful work from you. I have all eternity but you don't. I'm so sorry to have to remind you.

Vincent

(sarcastically)

Thanks a bunch. That's made me feel a whole lot better.

I'm not questioning your right to ask questions about circles, just where you're going with it.

> **Key insight:**
>
> Circles are strong energetic shapes. Circles bring people together. Circles are efficient. And circles have a history of being used for rituals – including magic.

The power of stepping into a circle

Roxy

Well, you need to learn to be a wee bit more present and a lot less peering out into the future, don't you?

So we've established that circles have power.

Well, there's another type of energetic power they have.

You can define an imaginary circle in a certain way. Then you imaginatively step in; and receive the energy of that definition, receive information that's obvious intuitively; or, perhaps, comes as a symbol.

Circles to kick-start your imagination

For example, where would you like to go on your next vacation? Define a circle as that and step in.

Vincent

We're back in COVID lockdown.[4] We try not to think about travel.

Roxy

(Sigh)

Humans!
Please just play along and nominate somewhere.

Vincent

OK I've got it. I'm in the UK visiting family, in Brighton, at the Amex[5] before a home game.

Roxy

Perfect. So define a circle that's all of that. Imaginatively draw it out on the floor of your room and step into it. What do you get? How does it feel?

---

4 Roxy says:
This was indeed true at the time of writing but Vincent's only using COVID as a smokescreen to hide the fact that he didn't have any money at the time of writing. Good job he found me and knuckled down to help create this book, which will surely help him enjoy the vacation of his choice. If he can, He's a bit of a workaholic which is a good job really because I have sooo many books to write with him.

5 Roxy says:
The AMEX is the American Express Community Stadium located in a beautiful location on the edge of Brighton, UK. One side is in town and the other in gentle rolling downland. They play there because their old ground was sold to make way for shops. Humans!

Vincent

Oh, I'm getting brothers and nephews and maybe a niece. Harvey's beer – and that's a special treat as I hardly drink at home. Piglets Pantry prize winning pies. Then the stands. Full house, blue and white everywhere. I feel happy, excited and full of expectation. There's so much beautiful noise from the crowd.

Roxy

Fantastic.

Vincent

No it's crap. I just realized we're playing Burnley. The most boring team in the English Premier League[6].

Roxy

In the English Premier League? They're the most boring team in the galaxy. In the universe. And beyond. Across all time. space and dimensions. Oh yes, they have a reputation in the spirit world and it's appalling. But it's your fault – you should have been clearer in your definition of the circle.

It's a pattern with you isn't it?

Vincent

Yes, I did see a Brighton Burnley match on one of my trips, yes it was boring and they were so dirty, our players were lucky to escape a season-ending injury.

Roxy

I didn't mean Brighton-Burnley matches.

---

6 Roxy says:
What Vincent won't tell you, because it's so shameful is that in the course of revising this book, Burnley came to the AMEX and won. It was some comfort to Vincent that they are no longer the most boring team in the English Premier League by virtue of being relegated to the Championship. However, at the time of the final revision of this book, they had won promotion back to the Premier League, and then dropped like a stone to the bottom three. Who knows where they'll be by the time you get to read this.

Humans!

I meant not defining circles precisely enough.

But would you agree you got a powerful energetic experience from stepping into that circle?

Vincent

Yes.

Roxy

And you don't even have to use a finger to draw the circle in front of you and physically step in. You can just imagine the circle and imagine yourself stepping into it.

Circles for guidance

You can use it to get guidance intuitively about anything you want.

Like what question do you want an answer to right now? One that's been burning you up for days?

Vincent

Well, I guess it's when will this lockdown in Melbourne end?

Roxy

That's not ideal. Using intuition for guidance into the future is fine but to just plain read the future and make predictions is very advanced and best avoided.

However, just this once, we'll work with that.

Vincent

OK. I get late November 2021.

Roxy

No editing that out when you revise the book OK? Even though the answer to your question is fairly predictable.

(sigh)

> **Key steps for using circles**
>
> 1. Decide what you need guidance on.
> 2. Come into innosense.
> 3. Imagine a circle.
> 4. Define it as informing you about what you need guidance on.
> 5. Intend to receive powerfully what's obvious or a symbol.
> 6. Consciously step in.
> 7. Interpret what you get. Consider the circle as a gateway to a flow of intuition. So you may be speaking or writing. Keep interpreting and be prepared to use your imagination to make it up.

Circles for decisions

And finally, you can use circles to help make decisions.

There was a training you were offered today. So define the circle as the truth of you taking that training and step in. What do you get?

Vincent

I got a detailed visual but the interpretation of that is emptiness. I get not to take the training. I get that there's nothing there for me. I don't get that it's bad in any way or dangerous. It's just that it's not true for me to use my time, money, and energy to take it.

Roxy

Very good VG. You made the decision simply, easily and without having to resort to lists of pros and cons, checking the funding or checking your availability. It was very simple.

Now, Flow Posse, there's more information and an exercise on circles in the online training that comes with the book. They are simple to talk about, simple to use, and so so powerful. Vincent has put all the links in Appendix 1

Exercises and resources.

> **Key insight:**
> You can get guidance on a decision by following the steps and defining the circle as the truth of the particular course of action you're considering or of one of the alternatives for a with either/or decision.

Summary

So, Vincent, please summarize this for me.

Vincent

Circles are a powerful way to obtain information through intuition.

You simply define an imaginary circle to give you the information you seek, come into innosense and connect with your intuition and then, in your imagination, you step into it.

You will receive a powerful energetic sense of what's going on in this circle and the information that's available to you from intuition.

Roxy

Very good, very good.

So, now we need to learn about the relationship between your higher and your unconscious, shadow.

Chapter 16

Your shadow

'Until you make the unconscious conscious, it will direct your life and you will call it fate.' – Carl Jung[7]

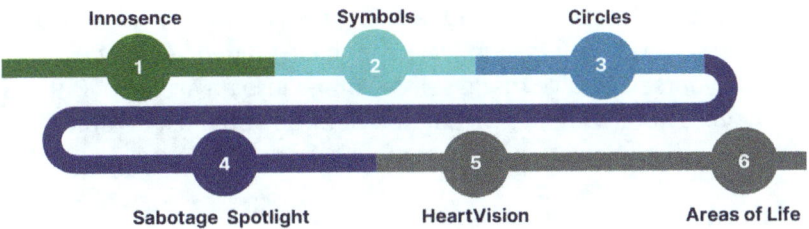

Why humans are so good at self-sabotage?

Roxy

Every one of you humans has a shadow – and I'm not talking about the sort that's created by the sun or lights. It's about that unconscious part of you that runs your life by default. It's that part of you that causes self-sabotage. However, most of you humans cannot see it so you're not even aware it exists.

---

7 Vincent says:
This is the popular version of the quote. The original quote reads:
'The psychological rule says that when an inner situation is not made conscious, it happens outside, as fate. That is to say, when the individual remains undivided and does not become conscious of his inner opposite, the world must perforce act out the conflict and be torn into opposing halves.'
- ~Carl Jung, Aion, Christ: A Symbol of the Self, Pages 70-71, Para 126

That's precisely why you humans are so good at sabotaging yourselves. Especially you, Vincent. You get resistance. That's the discomfort you feel that makes you avoid taking the action you know you should. You get distracted. Notifications, messages, ideas. Your world is full of them. They catch your eye and give you some fleeting pleasure as you give them your attention.

Vincent

What's up with you today? We're two paragraphs in and you're picking on me already.

Roxy

I'm sorry, Vincent, but you're such an easy target. And it's true. You sabotage yourself in ways that have eluded years of work on yourself. You've made self-sabotage into an art form. But you're here with me, writing the book so you must be doing something right.

Vincent

(grudgingly)
Thanks Roxy. Now can we get on with it?

Roxy

Certainly. So those of you that are parents, you may think being a parent is all about driving your children to sports or friends; or making sure they have something better than junk food to eat or making sure they're doing their homework and not just playing computer games. If you're a really good parent, it may be because you've read the parenting books, you follow the articles in the newspapers and you research it online; or perhaps you have good role models.

Childhood Wounding

What they don't tell you is that part of the journey of being a human parent is wounding your kids.

Vincent

You know how the Flow Posse are going to take that? I can see them thinking, 'Is Roxy seriously asking me to go out and buy a baseball bat or, worse, a golf club or something similar?' It's certainly not something you find in any parenting book or articles.

Roxy

Vincent! Credit your readers with a modicum of intelligence. At least, up to a point – you're all humans. And I'm sure they haven't taken that the wrong way.

I don't mean that as parents you get to indulge in any form of physical, verbal, emotional or even sexual abuse. Of course not. Although, regrettably, many – too many parents do that. And I'm quite certain that some of the Flow Posse have been on the receiving end.

No. It's just how you humans are created. The ancients used to say that the role of the mother was to nurture the baby – where else do they get food in the first weeks of their life? And the role of the father is to acknowledge their children.

When you're a baby, you want far more nurturing than Mamma can ever give. And every parent will remember those sleep-interrupted nights and the sleep-deprived days that followed and how tired and ratty you get. No wonder there are times when Mamma can't provide everything that you want and you feel that.

Moreover, a new baby brother or sister may turn up and demand Mamma's attention and take it away from you. Anything like that happen to you, Vincent?

Vincent

Well, yes. I'm the eldest of seven, and my next brother down came along a couple of weeks after I turned one year old. People who have given me readings often pick up on that wounding. As long as I remember, I've always been asthmatic; and more than one of those readings clarified that it all started around the age of one year old. The asthma, in turn, was a way to demand my mother's attention which I must have felt being withdrawn. But, of course, I could never get the attention I had before; hence the wounding.

Roxy

It surprises you, sometimes, what intuition turns up, doesn't it? Even though you know it shouldn't.

Then, as you grow into little preschoolers, all you want is attention from your father. You need to be acknowledged for who you are and for your potential in life. And you preschoolers can be extraordinarily demanding. And when you don't get that acknowledgement, you feel that too.

Often, you may have siblings competing for Mamma and Daddy attention.

And it all creates wounds to your psyche whether it's simple lack of nurturing and acknowledgement, serious dysfunction in one of your parents, for example, through alcohol or drugs, dysfunction in your parents' relationship – arguing, fighting, one parent abusing the other, or abuse.

And here's the key. As a young child, you take it personally. You make it about yourselves. After all, Mamma and Daddy are like gods to you. And so you make up stories about yourselves, perhaps that you're not worthy of Mamma's attention or perhaps whatever you do is never good enough to please Daddy.

> **Key insight:**
> It is impossible for human parents to give the young child all they want.
>
> The mother cannot give it all the nurturing and attention it needs and the father can never give it enough validation. This is our childhood wounding.
> To understand this, in our childhood, we make up stories about ourselves and why what we experience is our fault.

Limiting beliefs and compensating behaviors

Vincent

> You make it sound uncannily like those ancient religions where the people used to live in fear of angering their gods. And so they spent large chunks of their lives appeasing them with sacrifices and offerings.

Roxy

> Exactly. That's such a good analogy. And so you take that story you made up and create a belief about yourself and you start to compensate. You create behaviors designed to get you the nurturing or acknowledgement that's missing. For example, imagine a child who feels and believes that they are undeserving or unworthy, how would they behave and why?

Vincent

> They'd become a people pleaser? Trying to get the attention they crave, even at the expense of their own happiness?

Roxy

> Very good VG. And a child who never feels or believes that they are good enough because their father withholds acknowledgement?

Vincent

> They'd try and become an achiever to get noticed? Whether it's in sport or academics, arts and crafts, always trying to achieve or create or just be even more because who they are and what they've achieved in never recognized?

Roxy

> Very good again.
>
> And every sibling has a different experience because of where they are in the family and what their parents' availability and expectations are at the time,
>
> You humans all exit early childhood with these core beliefs and they are the nucleus of your shadow. You add to them each and every time you experience a hurt or a setback and you build that shadow nice and big and strong. And along with that, the limiting beliefs you have formed and the compensating behaviors that flow from those beliefs become ingrained. And then, when you get to adulthood, they become the cause of your self-sabotage. Often you have no idea why your relationships are so challenging, why you don't get that job you want, why your grand plans fail so miserably, why you seem plagued by setbacks that seem so random. Even why you have health issues.
>
> You may ask why all of this? Why is life so full of that quiet desperation Thoreau talked about? Why does it all have to be so hard?

> **Key insight:**
> From your childhood wounding, you create beliefs, assumptions and definitions that limit how you express yourself and that cause you to create challenging circumstances in your life.

Why the shadow?

Vincent

You've got the answer? I'd love to hear it.

Roxy

Of course I've got the answer. What else would you expect?

And, yes, I'll start to unfold it for you ...

In a nutshell, it's because, here in the spirit world, everything is beautiful and easy and filled with light and streaming energies; and yet we cannot create the amazing things you humans do.

Remember those images of heaven from your childhood books and stories?

Vincent

Of angels sitting around for eternity singing God's praises?

Roxy

Yes, and what did you think of that?

Vincent

I wondered wouldn't that be just a little bit boring? Who'd want to be an angel?

Roxy

Yes, and what do you think of that now?

Vincent

Well, then I experienced how powerful and joyful and easy chanting was in Kundalini Yoga.

Roxy

Indeed. And you went for ninety minutes once. Ninety whole minutes chanting the one mantra. That's not bad; but it's a long, long way from eternity.

Vincent

It was beautifully uplifting though. But I guess we're human and had to stop at some point.

Roxy

Exactly. We spirits can go for as long as we want, even eternity and it gets better and better – and even better.

But we can't create or expand or evolve in the way the physical universe does – and if we want to connect with that, we have to become human.

The key is that creation cannot come out of pure love and light. There has to be an opposing force, a challenge of some sort. Sometimes you create from the depths of that challenge, sometimes from the fear of it, sometimes from the joy or relief of overcoming it, and sometimes, just in spite of it – but always reaching for that which is higher and more creative. There's an Einstein quote going round your internet,
"No problem can be solved from the same level of consciousness that created it." Now it may be one of those many fake Einstein quotes that flood your internet that he never actually said, but there's still is truth in it.

That is why being human is so challenging. It gives you the opportunity to become great, to expand to create new ideas and works that have never existed before.

But in order to get that, you have to experience challenges; most of the challenges originate in your shadow.

> **Key insight:**
> As humans living in a physical world, you have the opportunity to become great, to expand to create new ideas and works that have never existed before, and to live to our true potential. However, in order to experience this growth, you also have to experience challenges; and most of the challenges originate in your shadow.

How do we deal with challenge?

Vincent

Do some people get overwhelmed with challenge?

Roxy

Some of you join one of those branches of Buddhism where you do everything to eliminate challenges in your life by eliminating desires and just staying present. But if challenge and growth are two sides of the same coin, eliminating challenge also eliminates the opportunity for growth and self-expression.

Some of you do get overwhelmed, depressed and, regrettably, even choose to end their lives.

And some of you learn to work with challenges so that you thrive in your lives. It does take a modicum of effort and we will shortly unveil a tool that will help you with this.

Key insight:
Some humans choose to try and eliminate challenge but this also limits their opportunities for growth.

Some of you deal with challenge by getting angry or going into denial or going into depression.

And some of you learn to work with challenge and enjoy the personal growth that comes as a result.

Limiting beliefs give rise to patterns of behavior

Many of you drift through life creating more challenges for yourselves as you go because you don't recognize the power of your shadow. Your compensating behaviors become your everyday behaviors, driven by those underlying beliefs laid down in childhood. Those create outcomes that reinforce your underlying beliefs. And it also causes patterns in your behavior.

A great example is known as the Karpman drama triangle.

There's a victim with the dysfunctional program laid down in childhood; 'I'm suffering. Poor me! But if I can make people see how much I'm suffering they'll give me support and love'.

And this pattern persists into adulthood. So they go out and create or find persecutors. They actually uinconsciously seek out people who will make them suffer in some way.

Can you believe that? It happens.

It could be another family member, the government, their boss, even a barista. Persecutors are everywhere. They're very easy to find. Then the victim can enlist one or more rescuers to give them a lot of support and love. That's the payoff. It's highly dysfunctional behavior but, like all dysfunctional behaviors, it does have a powerful payoff.

Now the rescuers feel they are doing the right thing in supporting the victim. It looks like and feels like a beautiful supportive thing to do. But the rescuer rarely understands that they are actually being used to perpetuate the drama.

And worse, if and when the drama somehow resolves, the victim goes ahead and creates more of the same. The barista made such a terrible coffee, I'm never going back there says the victim. And then they find another café where the coffee is good but the service is terrible. You know people like this don't you, Vincent?

Vincent

Yes I do; but don't expect me to name them. They might sue me. That would make them the victim and me the persecutor. And give them another way to get support.

Roxy

You're certainly on the ball today, Vincent. Very good.

Yes, for you humans, your shadows create patterns of behavior that repeat over and over again all the way through your life. And it is often much more serious than ever being able to find a café the victim likes. Ever wonder why family feuds always seem to drag out for so long? A lot of the time it's because the victim does not want to let go of the dysfunctional payoff, the support they get from rescuers.

It's as if every day is Groundhog Day for you humans. So sad.

> **Key insight:**
> Your limiting beliefs create patterns of behavior that repeat over and over.

So how do you deal with a challenge in a way that's in flow?

So how can you deal with a challenge in a way that's in flow?

Vincent

Is that one for me to answer? Or just a rhetorical question? I never know with you…

Roxy

Rhetorical this time, although I'm certain you'd come up with a good answer – if I pushed you hard enough.

Have you noticed how you humans have things that happen to you over and over?
Like the victim we just talked about.

Or that friend of yours who saw all her relationships fizzled in three to six months – until she found out that she had a pattern based on the belief men can't be trusted. So she'd test them and they'd pass. Then she'd raise the bar and test them again. And she'd repeat it until they left her – and proved her belief that men can't be trusted.

Funny how that works isn't it?

Vincent

It wasn't very funny for her. I think frustrating is the word you're after.

Roxy

But she's not like that anymore. What changed?

Vincent

She became aware of her behavior and beliefs and that pattern. And from there, it became quite easy for her to catch herself in the behavior; and then change it from a behavior based in her childhood belief system to an empowered adult behavior.

Roxy

You make getting out of these patterns sound so simple. It is, when you're aware of them. And the patterns are ingrained in the human condition. You have these childhood wounds and beliefs that run – and often ruin your life. What if you could become aware of them and the behaviors they create? What if you had the chance to short-circuit them and take away their power?

You'd think most humans would want that badly, wouldn't you?

Vincent

That would make sense.

Roxy

Yes, of course it would make sense. There is much wisdom in common sense. What a shame that you humans pay it lip service while your shadow runs your life.

Your dysfunctional patterns are so, so addictive. That's why so many of you humans are afraid of any training or tool that might show you up. You'd have to face your dysfunctions and own them. And the dysfunctions feel so comfortable because they seem to be keeping you safe. Whereas, they don't now and they didn't in childhood. They come from stories you made up about yourself; and those stories were never real.

It's such a shame because it's so easy for you humans to break out of your patterns. They have trigger points – you catch yourself doing this or you catch yourself feeling that. Once you catch yourself dropping into the behavior or the feeling, you just choose to let it go, to take a different course of action (or even inaction) and disengage the pattern completely. That's all you have to do.

> **Key insight:**
> The key to managing challenges is to bring awareness to your unconscious beliefs, assumptions, and definitions, to the behaviors that come from those, and especially to the triggers that push you deep into a space where your unconscious controls our lives. When you catch yourselves dropping into that, you can choose a different course of action.

So how do we become aware of our dysfunctional unconscious behaviors?

Vincent

So how do we become aware of our dysfunctional unconscious behaviors?

Roxy

You use a Sabotage Spotlight process – I do like my new name for it. It helps you analyze an occasion when you didn't get what you wanted and shows up how your dysfunctional self – your beliefs, assumptions and definitions created that.

Vincent

How are we going to demonstrate this?

Roxy

I'm going to do one on you.

Vincent

No. You can't do that.

Roxy

Why ever not?

Vincent

I don't want this in a book where my failings and weaknesses will be shown up in front of everybody. Surely you've chosen to work with me on this because it has a message that's not to be kept small; it's for a wide audience. You'd make me look bad and destroy my confidence and authority.

Roxy

Of course, of course.

(sigh)

I won't make you uncomfortable, at least on this occasion.

Please just answer this question – what's the cause of writer's block?

Vincent

That's easy. Self-censorship. Unwillingness to be vulnerable. Getting great ideas but blocking them because you don't want to write them down.

Roxy

And why do you humans want to self-censor?

Vincent

To avoid being judged, I guess,

Roxy

And what do you need to do to get over writer's block?

Vincent

Vulnerability. Openness.

Roxy

And what are you doing right now?

Vincent

What does it look like? You talk, I write it down. I'm doing the physical work of writing this book.

Roxy

Which means?

Vincent

I'm being vulnerable?

Roxy

Exactly. So as you've opened yourself up to some judgment, why can't there be a wee bit of ridicule as well?

Vincent

Thanks a billion. I'm not doing it.

Roxy

I talk, you write it down. That's what you said. If you won't give the answers to the questions in the process, I'll get them telepathically or perhaps just make them up.

Vincent

It's not going to happen. You know I can end the writing session whenever I want.

And right now, as it happens, I'm busting.

Roxy

That's only worth a two-minute break. Off you go. And make sure you come back!

...

Feeling better?

The Sabotage Spotlight process

Vincent

Relieved – but still on edge.

Roxy

So how long is it since you last worked on this book?

Vincent

Over a week. I was actually pretty shocked when I saw the version date.

Roxy

And what did you want?

Vincent

I have a target of four sessions per week. I obviously haven't been making it recently.

Roxy

Why not?

Vincent

I write in the late evenings and somehow they've all been evaporating lately. One evening was a late night coaching session with an overseas client. I lost a couple of evenings because Ratu[8] passed away in the week and the evening shakes have been going much longer. I lost one evening because I had to watch a few training videos before the following day.

Roxy

I think I've heard enough of the sob story. How did that make you feel?

---

8 Vincent says – Ratu Bagus, was the founder of shaking meditation – as in a previous footnote.

Vincent

Disappointed. Discouraged as well because this book is crying out to be written and I'm not making progress. I'm annoyed and frustrated with myself.

Roxy

So what does all that mean about you?

Vincent

This book is important to me and I'm not allowing myself to prioritize it. I feel like I'm a victim of the circumstances which have been dictating progress over the past week. Sort of powerless.

Roxy

OK and what does it mean about the other people in your life? Your friends and family?

Vincent

They don't care. This has nothing to do with them. They're like extras on a film set.

Roxy

And the world?

Vincent

Right now, the world doesn't know about this book and it doesn't care. And I just had a goosebumps moment – you, my guides, the universe all do care and want it published!

Roxy

Of course we do. That's why I'm here with you. And yet you're telling yourself the world doesn't care. Humans!

So what's the assumption underlying why you didn't get that time to work with me?

Vincent

Actually, I think it's that ...
I can't make the progress I'd like to on this book because don't have the capacity to free up time to write by managing my time; and I'm powerless to handle external demands on it.

Roxy

What behavior does that result in?

Vincent

I end up doing what I think everybody else thinks I should be doing and putting this book way down the priorities for time.

Roxy

And what's the result of that behavior?

Vincent

I miss my progress targets.

Roxy

So what would you love?

Vincent

I'd love to have this book done. Published. I'd love it to be out there in the world, talking about it and promoting it.

Roxy

And you know what action you need to take for that to happen?

Vincent

Start by getting back to four sessions a week.

Roxy

Four sessions a week? Four sessions a week? Surely you can do better than that?

Vincent

I'll have a look at it. Once my training project is set up, it should be easier.

Roxy

And there, ladies and gentlemen, you have it.

That is the Sabotage Spotlight process, Roxy-style.

The starting point is where we went for something and didn't get what we wanted.

First, we ask for thoughts or, as I call them, ejacs – excuses, justifications, arguments, and collusions[9]. Thoughts from the shadow.
Next, it's feelings or fadddds. Fears, anger (and frustration), disappointments, discouragement, disillusionment, depression

Then we identify your definitions – what you think those thoughts and feelings mean about you, others, and the world and even the universe.

And then we get to the bottom line, the underlying assumption. This is why you didn't get what you wanted (and don't get it in similar situations); and the answer to this has to be based on your underlying beliefs and definitions that have come up and sabotaged you. For this process, you can't put the blame on another person or circumstances. They may be partly to blame but you contributed in a major way; and if you hadn't the whole dynamic would be different. This is about how you sabotaged getting what you wanted.

From that we determine the behaviors and outcomes that you create from those beliefs and definitions.

---

9 Roxy says =
Collusions are when you find somebody else to listen to you and buy into your sob story. Sometimes they'll just pretend in the name of being supportive. Other times, they'll dive into their own dysfunction and join in the litany of complaints, criticism and grievances and you'll enjoy a conversation that you call supportive. Humans!

Getting into the Flow

And finally, we look at what you'd really love, ask where to from here? And find the action you need to take to move forward.

What the process shows up are the limiting belief(s) that are creating the unwanted outcome. And now you know what they are, Vincent, you can catch yourself before they catch you.

Voilà.

How painful was that?

Vincent

Actually, I'm feeling a bit of relief. I'm looking forward to getting back to moving forward with the book.

Roxy

Wonderful. Although I have to say I'm surprised that you're surprised about the outcome.

Now, Flow Posse, Vincent has put together some materials online that you can use to run your own Sabotage Spotlight processes. You'll find the links in Appendix 1 Exercises and resources.

And as one of his clients said yesterday, 'he has a very soothing voice'. And an English accent – what more could you want?

> The steps to the Sabotage Spotlight process are listed in Appendix 1 Exercises and resources.

So Vincent, tell us again why is this process so important?

Vincent

It shows up our dysfunctional behaviors and the beliefs and definitions that drive them – and, interestingly, those same beliefs will keep showing up no matter what area of life we look at, stopping us from getting what we want.

It helps us identify when we're slipping into those behaviors and choose a better course of action.

Roxy

Very good, VG. You have earned your cocoa tonight.

Vincent

And some of those dried almonds as a snack.

Roxy

Even though you've chosen to be doing intermittent fasting.

(Sigh)

Humans!

Vincent

True. Most evenings I feel powerless to resist a little snack. But tonight's different.

Or is it?

I feel like I've really earned them.

Roxy

Powerless? Where have I heard that before?

Humans!

I think that makes it time for you to summarize, Vincent.

> **Key insight:**
> The Sabotage Spotlight process shows up your dysfunctional behaviors and the beliefs, assumptions and definitions that drive them. It makes the unconscious conscious and helps you understand how you sabotage yourselves.

Summary

Vincent

> We humans have an unconscious that is mostly hidden from us and that we have to work to make conscious.
>
> The unconscious is built on the limiting beliefs we create in childhood as we try to make meaning from the wounding we receive from our parents.
>
> The Sabotage Spotlight process shines a light on this and shows up the unconscious beliefs running our lives, undermining progress towards our goals and what's on our vision boards.

Roxy

> So now you're good to make your goals and end results?

Vincent

> Well, not exactly. Don't we also need to dispense with any goals that come from our unconscious, from that wounding, from any inner place of lack and replace them with choices that align with our greatness and purpose?

Roxy

> Then get into the flow and create the end results you truly desire?
>
> That's coming up next.
>
> So, Flow Posse, take a short break guys, get a cuppa, stretch your legs and come back to this with a fresh mind. After all, you're only human.

Part 5

Putting the tools to work

Chapter 17

Alignment

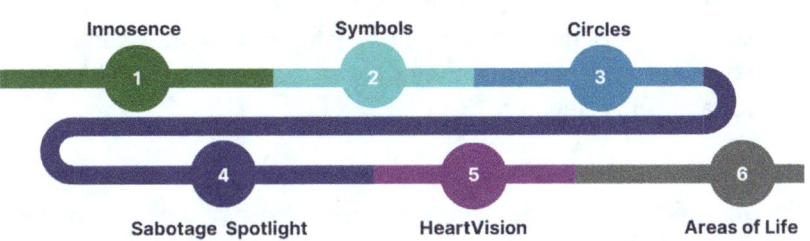

Goals, plans and choices

Roxy

> Let's talk about goals, today. You humans have many personal development gurus and they all start by talking at length about the importance of goals and about how all the high achievers in the world start by setting goals. Wouldn't you say that's true Vincent?

Vincent

> That all high achievers set goals and work towards them? Pretty much. There are a few exceptions I can think of. People like Mother Teresa, who achieved great work in their lives but didn't start out with a goal of doing that. There are a few others that stumbled on their path by luck – or perhaps, synchronicity. But most high achievers do set goals.

Roxy

So, what could possibly go wrong with setting goals and working towards them?

Vincent

Well, some people make their goals but many people don't. Jerry Hicks co-founded the Abraham-Hicks work. Before that, he used to teach using Napoleon Hill's book *Think And Grow Rich*. He saw some people do well and get rich, but many seemed to fail no matter how many times they attended his course or how diligently they worked. So he moved on looking for answers elsewhere.

Roxy

Yes, and with you, you've been one of those people that never quite seem to make it, despite all your hard work. Haven't you? Be honest.

Vincent

Please don't embarrass me.

Roxy

I'm not trying to embarrass you, Vincent. It would be so much worse for you … so much worse … if I did.

I asked that question with love. Tough love.

Missing goals is just what happens with many of you humans.

The interesting question is, if you've set your goals, what could possibly go wrong?

Vincent

Lots of things could go wrong.

The person setting the goals may not have the skills or knowledge to execute their plan. There are often actions they'd need to take that are totally missing from their plans because they were never even aware of them. They may have what they think is a wonderful idea but nobody else agrees or is prepared to invest in it or to pay for their product or service. Or some major random external event may come along and totally change the market environment and what they were planning to do is no longer wanted. Or a technology change comes in that makes the goal they were working on obsolete.

Roxy

Was that just a memory dump of your goals that you failed to make? Or are you in the flow today, Vincent?

Vincent

Sometimes it's hard to work with a know-it-all, telepathic spirit guide. Are you planning to go through all my dirty laundry? And I mean that metaphorically.

Roxy

Vincent, do you really think I need to be told it was a metaphor? As if I'd be interested in the contents of your laundry basket. Humans!

However, you can breathe a sigh of relief. I'm not going to pick apart all of your failed goals, one by one, in detail. That would take a whole other book. So I'll spare you any more embarrassment – at least for today.

Anyway, your Flow Posse will be curious. According to most of your gurus, you humans have to set goals to achieve highly. And, while some of you do end up making those goals, many of you don't. Tell me, why would you set goals that you're not likely to make?

Vincent

I'd say because most of our goals end up coming from the dysfunctional part of ourselves; our places of pain and lack – and those places are painful. So our goals tend to express yearnings for what we lack, like money, time, freedom, or even self-esteem. The typical goal-setting exercise asks you how you'd like your life to be. Visualize the mansion and the car, the private jet for example. Or what qualifications you want.

> **Key insight:**
> Most goal-setting programs ignore where your goals come from. By default, your goals will come from your unconscious and your conditioning; from a place of lack and neediness. So when you go to create the results of those goals, you give power to the unconscious; and it sabotages them.

Roxy

And what could possibly be wrong with setting goals for more time, money or freedom?

Vincent

Well, those are goals that are created from our shadow. They come from trying to ease the pain of our wounding, to gain the approval of those around us and compensate from the beliefs that come out of all that. Perhaps we have a need to be impressive, or perhaps we feel not good enough.

So when we create those goals, we're unconsciously telling ourselves that our shadow created them. We're telling ourselves that's where the power is in our consciousness.

And so, because the shadow has the power, it sets us up to sabotage ourselves.
And that, in turn, confirms our limiting beliefs.

Roxy

Very good, VG.

Vincent G. Melling

I often think you humans set S.M.A.R.T[1] goals to make you feel smart because you can say, 'I have SMART goals'. It sounds impressive. But in reality it just gives you five ways to fail.

And something else with goals – if or, rather, when you sabotage yourself and fail to make a goal, you reinforce the story about yourself and about what a failure you are at life.

You used to get that a lot didn't you Vincent?

Vincent

Well, a bit.

Roxy

I said a lot. Humans!

And something else – you make goals time-bound. Now that works where the timing is predictable – for example something you've done before or for something like a university course with set timing. Or the time you get away from work at the end of the day – most people have that as a top goal, even if it's not actually on their list of goals. But what about when you're doing something new that you've never done before?

You can be making good progress but then something unforeseeable – or, more often, something that was totally foreseeable and that you overlooked occurs, which causes you to miss your goal date. And that makes you a failure.

And you know you set yourself up for that, which makes it a double-failure.

Humans! How ridiculous!

There's a part of you that knows that most goal dates are

---

1 Roxy says SMART stands for Specific, Measurable, Achievable, Relevant and Time-bound. Like many management tools of the late 20th century, the purpose of SMART goals is to shift the blame – and accountability – from management to their workers – even though management control the scope, measures, resources, and acceptable timelines.

Getting into the Flow

completely arbitrary, not driven by any external constraint, so missing the goal date isn't that big a deal.

One last thing, Vincent. Goals need to be achievable. But how so you humans define achievable?

Vincent

Perhaps it's a result you've created before. Perhaps it's a goal where you have experience of completing all the steps. You would have confidence that you have all the resources you need – the time, the people, the money, the help and mentoring to get it done.

Roxy

So often, you humans limit yourselves to setting only those goals that you believe are achievable.

That's so sad. That's so limiting, indeed. It means that you won't go for something that your heart and soul (and/or your intuition) are crying out for but that you deem to be unrealistic.

Why don't you humans just settle for wishes?

Vincent

I guess because ... unless you have a fairy godmother, they hardly ever come true.

Roxy

Exactly. And then, you humans often end up settling for wishes anyway and then hope because wishes and hope don't actually require you to take any action.

You humans believe you won't get what you want. But you don't know any better.

What about plans?

Vincent

Plans are like goals – sometimes they don't work out because life gets in the way.

Often they get done but with a lot more effort and taking a lot more time than you originally planned for.

And for some people, their plans never come to anything.

Roxy

Ah Robert Burns – 'the best laid plans of mice and men'...

Vincent

Don't tell me. You wrote that.

Roxy

I did not. He did. He was too busy chasing human women to have time for a muse.

Choices

So instead of working with wishes and hopes, goals and plans, you humans need to learn to work with choices. And a choice is where you select one possible future, out of all the possibilities and focus on that like a laser beam.
It's chosen.
And at the same time, every other possible outcome is not chosen. That is a pretty clear message to the universe, is it not?

> **Key insight:**
> Hopes, wishes, intentions, goals, plans, all inherently open up the possibility of ending up without your desired end results. This is why we work with choices as they are simply a decision - a selection of a single possible future.

Next you need to learn to receive your choices from your intuition, from what your heart and soul truly desire to be in your life, not from your shadow, your place of pain and lack.

AND, when you do, your choices will be about what you truly want in your life from your greatness, your higher self, your soul. They will articulate your highest potential in life, and even the agenda that you set yourself as a soul before you began your journey into physicality. In many, no most cases, your shadow will try and tell you that you can never have them. And you're going to create them anyway.

How does that sound?

Vincent

Most humans would say 'BS. I know what I want and its lots of money and I want it now'.

Roxy

(deep sigh)

You're right, Vincent. Humans!

And a truly miniscule proportion of you will ever end up getting that money. At a deep level, you all know that too but you are in denial.

We are here to change all that.

We're here to help our Flow Posse create extraordinary lives from their intuitive vision, and show the rest of humanity what you can all achieve. How does that sound?

Vincent

You know I love that. It has opened up so many possibilities in my life. But most humans would still say, 'But I want the money and I want it now'.

Roxy

Humans! But-heads!

Your thinking is so limited. And you judge what you think you can do and cannot do.

This is about how you humans can all get into the flow of the universe and co-create with it ...
... and what you can co-create with the universe, with a little magic, or a lot, is way beyond what your mind considers you

are capable of creating.

... which in turn is way beyond what your shadow would allow you to create – especially if you don't know how to catch it limiting you,

... which in turn is way beyond what you will actually create if your shadow is in control

... which, may I remind you, for you humans, happens to be your default. And, let me remind you, by default, what you create ends up being the proof of the dysfunctional belief from which your goal was set and not the goal itself.

Got it?

Vincent

Could you repeat all that?

Roxy

Why? It's a book. You and your Flow Posse can just read it over a couple of times until it really sinks in.

Vincent

How about an example?

Roxy

That would be good – but be careful what you ask for...

Tell me about your original house goal from way back when you first learned about goal setting.

Vincent

The large manor-style house, in the country but still close to the city, with the helipad?

Roxy

Keep going.

Vincent

And the helicopter and the luxury cars and the large kitchen and not much about the interior but very impressive anyway.

Roxy
> Impressive?

Vincent
> Yep. It turned out years later that one of my dysfunctional programs is the need to be impressive.

Roxy
> And you thought the helipad was kind of neat, didn't you?

Vincent
> It still is a neat idea, but not necessary, not part of my current vision for my home.

Roxy
> So what's that?

Vincent
> A spacious sun-filled home that grounds me, and supports my choices.

Roxy
> Interesting. Now it has a beautiful feeling and energy and it's about how you use the home to support your life.

Getting choices from the higher

> So, Flow Posse what you're going to do next is to create choices from your greatness, your genius, your higher self.
>
> And you're going to use imagination – true imagination that comes from your greatness, your genius, your higher self.
>
> We're going to go into innosense.
>
> Then we're going to take an imaginary journey to an imaginary place where everything your heart desires exists and you're going to write that down. We'll call that writing your HeartVision. Imagine it as an utopian place where everything

that's ever been true for you to create or experience is just waiting to reveal itself to you. This is the vision from your true greatness, your highest aspect, from your soul.

You can imagine the people that are there. Now, this isn't heaven, so don't go looking for Napoleon or JFK or John Lennon or other dead people. Although if they do turn up, then it's important. However, it is perfectly acceptable, even desirable, to see the people who are in your life already, family friends, people you work with; and they may have a new role in your life.
And you may meet new people who can help you create your end results.

You'll imagine the things you'd really love to create in your life. You might see a sailing trip. Other people would get seasick just thinking about it. It's very individual.

From there, your intuition may take you to other parts of the world.

Sometimes there are things like cars, homes, boats. Sometimes there are experiences – places to visit, activities, new practices. Sometimes there are skills, or personal qualities or ways of being – peaceful is a common one. Sometimes there are businesses. Sometimes there are artworks. You always get books don't you?

Vincent

Yes. Always books. Usually just the titles.

Roxy

Well, you don't have the time to write the whole book. Obviously. Consider how long this book is taking to write. It's significantly more than a journaling session, wouldn't you say?

> **Key insight:**
> To create choices from your greatness, your genius, your higher self, you need to get a vision from that place. Below, there is a link to an audio version online; and the key steps are listed in Appendix 1 Exercises and resources.

So now, Flow Posse, the exercise comprises a guided meditation and then writing or journaling. You'll need to set aside an hour to do it. Before you start, make sure you have a pad and a pen handy. Now please go off and do the HeartVision exercise using the audio that accompanies this book.
Here's the link (and all the links are listed in Appendix 1

Exercises and resources)
https://vincentgmelling.com/gitf-symbols-and-beyond

Chapter 18

Creating Choices

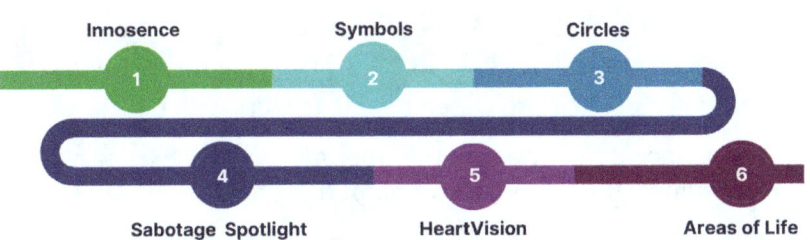

Building on the HeartVision

Roxy

So welcome back, Flow Posse.

I'm going to assume you've done the HeartVision exercise, and, if you haven't and you're just reading through, be sure to do it and come back here.

If you have done the meditation, you will have written out everything you got from that.
Wasn't it wonderful?
You now have your vision of what you'd love in your life from your heart and soul, there on paper in front of you. What an extraordinary gift to yourself! Congratulations! How many of you humans have that?

Vincent

Very few, I guess. Most of us that have done some sort of goal-setting exercise would now have a shopping list of goals from our limitations and shadows. This is so much more.

Roxy

That was a rhetorical question; but, well done, you still came up with a good answer anyway.

Don't think you're done just yet, though.

What would be the point of having this beautiful vision and writing it down if you weren't going to work with it?

And Vincent, that was another rhetorical question; However, this time, I do need you to attempt to respond.

Vincent

It's hard enough answering your real questions. Now you expect me to answer the rhetorical ones too.

Are you glaring at me again? I did answer that last one well enough — so you said.

OK no need to answer, I can see you are.

My response. Well, if our Flow Posse just stopped here, they'd have another beautiful guided meditation that had no practical impact on their lives after they opened their eyes at the end.

Roxy

Precisely. I couldn't have said it better myself. Actually, I could easily have come up with finer-sounding words but this is not poetry, it's a serious metaphysical text that comes to our Flow Posse with love. Tough love. So Vincent, what might that tough love involve at this stage?

Identify themes

Vincent

Well, Flow Posse, you need to start working with your journaled vision. You start by identifying themes from your writing.

Roxy

Themes eh? You make it sounds like a chore! No, it's exciting. Themes are what your intuition and true vision have shown you is important to you. It's from the perspective of your greatness. It's not a have-to-do list. It's a vision of your greatness unfolding.

So, what might be a theme that comes out of this journaled writing?

Vincent

Well, Flow Posse ...

Each element, each scene, everything you saw in your writing suggests one or more themes for what you'd love, what's true for you in your greatness in your life.

You may have seen a home or a community where you'd love to live, a business or the work you're called to; your soulmate, family or friends.

You may have seen physical things – a sailboat, a car, even wealth like a pile of money or a check.

Roxy

Do you humans still use checks? Still? Would you even know what they are?

Vincent

Some of us live in countries where they are still widely used and some of us are just old enough to remember them.

And please don't make me feel old, while you remind me how you're immortal. Again.

Roxy

I won't. You managed to do a good enough job of that yourself. Now carry on.

Vincent

So. Flow Posse, you may have seen an artwork or received a book title or several. Write those down. You may have sensed qualities about yourself, or perhaps a way of being. And you were given a gift when you entered the HeartVision. What does your intuition tell you it means?

You're looking for eight or nine themes.

Roxy

Not bad Vincent.

> **Key insight:**
> Your HeartVision journaling will have a number of elements or scenes –
>
> what you received. A theme is a grouping of related scenes that appear at first sight to come from a similar end result. There may just be onc scene in a theme or there may be multiple scenes – for example, a vision of sailing in a yacht might be linked to a part of the world you want to visit or to a home you want to create. Use your intuition to determine which scene(s) is/are related to a single theme.

Vincent

Not bad? Not bad?

I thought that was a pretty good run-down and all I get is like a pass grade?

Roxy

Humans! You said it yourself; you know your work was good. Why do you need me to validate that?

And don't answer that, Vincent. That's not for this book.

So now, Flow Posse, take some time to drop into innosense and then identify the themes in your HeartVision.

Don't over-think it. If you're over-thinking it, it means you've disengaged your intuition. Humans!
Just come back to innosense, reconnect with the excitement and fun of seeing your future unfold and continue. It's not rocket science. The themes should be self-evident, even to a human. Then come back to this book when you are done.

If you're really struggling to get to eight or nine themes, Vincent has created the 'Areas of Life' meditation to take you back into your HeartVision, identify what you may have missed in the original meditation, and expand your list.

You can access that in the same place as the HeartVision – here https://vincentgmelling.com/gitf-symbols-and-beyond

Stay with your themes until you have your eight or nine.

And I say that with love. Tough love...

Vincent

This is a book. We can't actually put music on for you to work with like we would in a workshop. But there is some online at the same link as above.

> **Key insight:**
> You will get very little from completing the HeartVision meditation unless you use it to create your choices to set your direction in life. The first part of this work is to identify 8-9 themes.
>
> - First, create a bullet point list of things you saw or felt during the meditation.
> - Next, if you have a lot of bullet points, group the ones that you intuitively sense are related and these will be your themes.
> - Finally, if you have fewer than eight themes, use the Areas of Life meditation to revisit your HeartVision and find more. There is a link above to an audio version online; and the key steps are listed in Appendix 1 Exercises and resources.

Turning themes into choices

Roxy

Welcome back Flow Posse.

Now you're going to turn those themes into choices. You need these choices. They will steer your life in the direction of your heart's desire, your soul's agenda. As I said before, a choice is a selection of one possible outcome out of all the possible outcomes. As I've told you before, but it bears repeating – a choice is a statement to your consciousness and, through that to universal consciousness that of all the possible timelines in your future, this is the one you choose and no other. So the universe will start to co-create that with you. It knows where you want to get to and starts to rearrange timelines, the people, the resources, opportunities, and everything else necessary to get you there.

Now, Vincent, you tell them how to create choices because that's something you happen to be good at.

Vincent

I'd say very good, thank you very much.

Not that I need your validation.

Roxy

Yes, yes, very good. Very good VG.

Now please, please keep calm and carry on.

Vincent

OMG – did you write that?

Roxy

Actually, I did. Back in 1939. Five short words. One of my smaller jobs. It wasn't considered to be useful at the time and most of the print run got pulped. But it's time came eventually and it's been, let's say, most impactful, as you'd expect, wouldn't you agree?

Now get on with it.

Vincent

OK, this is how you derive choices from your theme;

Guideline #1 – all choices must be based on what you received from your intuition, your HeartVision. Trust that everything that you received was from your intuition and insight. Don't judge it.

And don't make choices that come from outside of this. Very occasionally, intuition will give you a new choice directly. Perhaps when you're lying in bed at night, out on a jog or gardening. It will have a ring of truth about it that's almost tangible, and you'll be left in no doubt that it came intuitively. But for now, we're using only what you received in HeartVision.

> **Key insight:**
> All themes and choices come from your HeartVision.

Roxy

Very good Vincent. And, Flow Posse, this is extremely important. Choices from intuition express what you want from your heart and soul, and you'll create from a place of love.

But, after everything we've said, some of you still create choices that are based in lack and no more than the opposite of something you lack or some problem you're trying to resolve. Humans! Why? If you have those choices, you'll simply create more of the lack, more of the problem. You have been warned.

Now, Flow Posse, pause your reading for a moment or two and just consider – or even better, use a circle to tune into what might be the end result of one of those choices that comes from lack. Use it to refine the end result, feel the emotion and sense the essence.

Did you pause and do the circle? Seriously? It only takes a few seconds.

In a workshop, Vincent would be asking what answers came through for you. But as this is a book – here it is. Choices that are based on your lack have their roots in your shadow, in your dysfunctional beliefs. That means that when you make a choice like that, you're giving the power to those beliefs and so you will perpetuate them. I choose the end result of lots of money – when it comes from a space of lack it will continue to perpetuate the poverty in your life. However, if you actually did see money, a pile of gold or a check in the HeartVision, then claim it and create a choice about it. It's rare but it happens. I know I sound like a broken record – and it is indeed fortunate that vinyl recordings keep making comebacks so that you understand the metaphor – but I do need to keep repeating it.

OK Vincent, Let's move on.

Vincent

Guideline #2 is don't worry about getting it right first time, just get it down. At this stage, don't worry about the length or the wording. Once you have something you can begin to feel the energy of it, tune into it, and revise it.

Guideline #3 is that all choices start with the words, "I choose the end result of...."

Guideline #4 – be sure to choose *an end result*, not a process. Some of you might choose to learn to play the piano or another musical instrument – that's a process. What would an end result of that be? Perhaps to pass a Board of Music exam which requires a certain level of skill; or perhaps to play a certain piece that you love.

> **Key insights –**
> Get a draft choice written down first and be prepared to revise it by tuning into the energy of your end result.
>
> All choices start with the words "I choose the end result of".
>
> Make sure you are choosing an end result, not a process.

Roxy

That's a good start. Choosing a process is a common mistake and so easy to fix.

Now how can your Flow Posse make their choices compelling?

Vincent

I was getting to that. Why do you keep interrupting?

Roxy

That's my job. Keeping you on track. Now please continue.

Vincent

Guideline #5 – ask yourself what's the core of your choice? What is it in a nutshell? What's the heart of it? What's it really about? What's the true end results? Most of the time, you'll find you can express the core of the choice in three or four key words. It helps strip away all the supporting detail you saw and get to the essence of the choice.

A good tool to use here is to go into innosense, define a circle as the end result of your choice and step into it and simply ask the question, what's the core of this choice?

Roxy

Like your choice of a breathtakingly beautiful retreat center. That is so evocative.

Vincent

Yep. That was a good one. And often intuition will help you revise the choice by dropping in the perfect words. Sometimes it will happen at a time you're not even working on choices. I've had the right words for a couple of my choices drop in when I was out running and used those to revise the wording of those choices.

Another example was my rather long-winded choice to create a charity to help the people I'd seen in Eswatini (formerly known as Swaziland). As one friend put it, they are Africa's third world.

Intuition told me that the choice in a nutshell was 'helping African kids'. That's what I really wanted to do. The charity is still in the choice list at the end. But the choice starts with the core words, 'I choose the end result of helping African kids.' For me, that evokes the smiles on their faces.

> **Key insights:**
> The core of a choice's end result can usually be expressed in three or four key words.

Guideline #6 – does the choice evoke the emotion of the end result? The joy or the fun or the reward? Because it's this emotion that will make it compelling. In some cases, the emotion is obvious to you from the core choice we got from guideline 6. Other times, you may need to add the emotion explicitly to the wording of the choice. I could have written "I choose the end result of the joy of helping African kids". That's just an example. I don't really need to add the word "joy" because I feel it anyway; but it demonstrates how you can add emotion if the choice lacks it.

Roxy

And this is important. It's the emotion of the choice that creates the power to your consciousness. If you don't connect to the emotion, then the choice will not convey a powerful message to your consciousness.
Carry on, Vincent.

> **Key insights:**
> Ensure that your choice evokes a strong sense of the emotion of the end result; for example you can add emotionally charged adjectives to the choice or you can explicitly mention the emotions in the choice, or maybe the core end result naturally connects you to those emotions.

Vincent

That leads to Guideline #7 – make it specific. This is about adding the detail that's necessary to accurately evoke your end result but not so much that it loses its impact. So in the choice of helping Africans kids by adding, "through my charity" transforms it from being vague to having a specific end result – of establishing a way to raise funds to support them, and starting to get money in.

A choice is not intended to be a full and complete specification of exactly what you want down to the finest detail – just enough for you to fully connect with the vision and emotion of what it is that you're creating.

Roxy

Very good VG. If you humans saw a house in your HeartVision, what was most important? Location? A style of house like a condo or apartment? A particular feature? We don't want our choice to be the real estate promotional version with the count of bathrooms, bedrooms, car spaces, the brand of the appliances and how close it is to the nearest shopping mall. You need to make your choices succinct so that they give clear and powerful messages to your consciousness. Long choices confuse it. Some of you will ignore this advice anyway. Humans!

Now there's nothing wrong if you saw all the detail in your HeartVision. It's just that your choice needs to be simplified. One way to do that is to ask yourself 'what's a deal breaker for this choice?' That will help you identify the one or two specifics without which you wouldn't be interested.

> **Key insight:**
> The core keywords will give you a sense of the end result but you may need additional key details to clarify and add specificity. However, be wary of making your choice into a lengthy shopping list!

Carry on Vincent.

Vincent

Guideline #8 – a key adjective or two can add emotion and make your choice more compelling. I could have just chosen the end result of a retreat center but those adjectives, "breathtakingly beautiful" really engage my imagination and give it so much more juice.

> **Key insight:**
> Use adjectives to add emotion

Guideline #9 – make sure there's tension.
I had a student once who chose a loving and supportive relationship with their soulmate. That was such a terrible choice for them.

Roxy

It sounds good at first sight; so perhaps you could explain to our Flow Posse.

Vincent

Because the student was choosing what they already had; so they're not compelled to create anything greater.

Roxy

Very good, Vincent. When current reality is close to or the same as the end result, there's no tension. It's like a rubber band that hasn't been stretched. Humans! What would you suggest they choose, Vincent?

Vincent

I suggested they tune into the next level of this choice; go back into their HeartVision and identify what they'd really love next in the relationship.

Roxy

Very good VG. Next?

> **Key insight:**
> The choice needs to create tension – so make sure that the end result is not too close to current reality.

Vincent

Guideline #10 – don't choose an end result that's too far out in the future. If you want to learn piano, then going from zero experience to passing your first exam or performing your first piece in front of an audience is a sizeable step but not too great a jump. However, unless you're already an advanced pianist, choosing to play Rachmaninoff's 3rd piano concerto, is so far away that it will trigger your shadow and beliefs powerfully and you'll give up before you even make a start. This is especially the case for business and artistic/creative choices.

> **Key insight:**
> An end result that's too far away could potentially trigger your shadow and end up building in sabotage. Look for something that's a little way beyond what you could reasonably expect to achieve. You should expect to revisit the HeartVision and repeat creating choices between 9 and 15 months; so wherever you get to with your initial 'make a significant start' choice, your long-term vision will come from a subsequent HeartVision.
>
> For example, if you see yourself playing a piano concerto and have never played before in your life, consider choosing an end result that would be a stretch for you to achieve in nine to fifteen months. When you repeat the HeartVision, if it is still true for you to play the concerto, you can choose a new end result that's a stretch from what you have achieved.
> Some skills will take years to develop and some end results will take years to create.

Guideline #11 – if the choice is about serving others, tune in to what they really want and what you're really giving and incorporate it. The choice must be about serving others, not about how it's making you look.

> **Key insight:**
> For choices about serving others, use a circle to tune in to what the people you serve want and ensure your choice is consistent with that.

Guideline #12 – Finally, try and get the choice as succinct as possible while retaining the essence.

> **Key insight:**
> Make the choice as succinct as possible while retaining its essence

That's all the guidelines.

Roxy

Very good VG...

Vincent

But I haven't finished.

Roxy

I'm sorry, you're not usually this talkative. Usually I struggle to get the words out of you, and they come dripping with attitude and now you are in this wonderful flow. I'm just not used to it.

Vincent

Thanks, Roxy. I can't quite believe you said that.

Roxy

I suppose I have to be careful not to let you get complacent.

(sigh)

Carry on.

Vincent

Ah, yes. There are two fundamental choices that we suggest everyone adds to the top of their list.

The first is;

I choose the end result of living my true nature and purpose.

It's choosing to embrace and receive your capacity as a creator and to live from that orientation rather than let your shadow run your life.

And the second one is;

I choose the end result of being healthy.

They're called fundamental choices because they set your orientation in life and underpin all the others.

> **Key insight:**
> Include these fundamental choices in your list :-
>
> I choose the end result of living my true nature and purpose.
>
> I choose the end result of being healthy.

Roxy

So what if some choices appear to come from both your vision and from lack or problems? Do you have anything like that?

Vincent

> Sure. Take that fundamental choice of being healthy. For me, that includes being a healthy weight. Do I have a weight problem I'd like to solve? Yes. Does that stop me from having a choice to be healthy? No.
>
> If it's in the HeartVision or covered by a fundamental choice, claim it, regardless of whether there is pain in your current reality or not. Just be sure to write it in a way that claims the vision and end result, and not one that's trying to get away from your current circumstances.
>
> And now I'm done Roxy.

> **Key insight:**
> A choice such that of a particular home might appear both in your HeartVision and be something you lack. If it appears in the HeartVisions, it's OK to choose it.

Roxy

> That's what you think. What if one of your Flow Posse wants more help?

Vincent

> It's usual for them to get one-on-one help with their choices and it's a great way to start working towards their end results.

Roxy

> So you recommend they get a coach? Why can't you say that yourself? Not seeing your own greatness? Again?
> Apart from help with choices, what else can coaching help them with?

Vincent

> Coaching gives clients accountability. Clients agree to take action and give an account in the next session. Those agreements serve to exert a powerful force in consciousness

that compel the client to take the actions and create the results they agreed to.

Coaching also gives clients reflection. It's not easy for anyone to see when they are sabotaging themselves until the sabotage has happened; and the coach can help not only by nipping sabotage in the bud but also by helping the client to an understanding of sabotage patterns, how it might show up and how to handle it.

And finally, coaching gives the clients the opportunity to learn advanced tools, techniques, and ideas as they need them. These are beyond the scope of this book and entry-level training.

Roxy

And?

Vincent

And what?

Roxy

Why do I have to spell everything out for you? How do they go about finding a coach?

Vincent

If they go to my website, they'll be able to get more information about my coaching program and how to join it.

Roxy

They can coach with you personally?

Vincent

Yes, if I feel that they're a fit and if I'm taking on new clients. I only have a limited number of slots.

Roxy

Because you don't like to work??

Vincent

Because I have to leave some time for all those books I'm going to write with you.

Here's the link for coaching enquiries;

https://vincentgmelling.com/vgm-coaching

Summary.

Roxy

Please summarize for us.

Vincent

(sighs)

Roxy

Oh. I know what you're thinking and you are just making mountains out of molehills, Vincent. AGAIN! You're not getting out of it. Summaries are not a lot of work. Please just do it.

Vincent

I'm tired Roxy. I'm only a human after all.

But before you get a chance to get back at me – again, here's the summary.

We create choices to steer our lives in the direction of our hearts desires, of what we want in our lives. They come from intuition only, through the HeartVision exercise. This gives us a set of themes which we can then turn into choices.

We need to avoid choices based in lack or to resolve a problem because that only perpetuates the lack or makes the problem worse.

And finally, we should expect to repeat the HeartVision exercise and choices every nine to fifteen months. As we create our end results, we can expect a new expanded vision to unfold for us.

Roxy

Sorry, but not sorry to disappoint you, Flow Posse. You will have to repeat this exercise in the future. We have explained why.

Vincent

What we have here is the opportunity to start creating what we truly love.

So don't miss out. Before we move on, please create your choices if you haven't done so already.

Chapter 19

Creative Tension

Alignment and creative structure recap

Roxy

So perhaps, Vincent, you'd like to remind us about the relationship between alignment and creative structure.

Vincent

Do I have to? Can't you? I'm tired tonight.

Roxy

Again? Humans!

(sigh)

You have no idea what it's like to never be tired. Few of you have any idea, no, I'll correct myself for once, any memory of what it's like to be full of energy and ready to go. Your little children do. You say it makes you tired just watching them. Then your children turn into teenagers and seem to think it's normal to sleep in till early afternoon. How quickly you forget you could ever have so much energy! You humans have forgotten that you can just turn the energy on whenever you want. Now I'll tell you how you can do this one day – but that's not for now.

Very well, I'll start then.

Alignment is about where you're going. When you're kayaking, it's aiming for that place at the end of the journey where you

Getting into the Flow

take the kayaks out of the water to load onto trailers to go home. So far, so good wouldn't you agree?

Vincent

Of course. Alignment is all about answering the questions, 'Where would I love to end up? What would I love to create? What direction should I be going in life?' All from a heart and soul perspective.

Roxy

'Wouldn't you agree?' only requires a 'Yes' or a 'No' answer. But I'll let that pass this time.

So, it's fantastic to have alignment and know where you're going in life. But that's just the start. Earlier in the book, we learned about structure and now we are going to put it to work.

Vincent

I remember that chapter. It was pretty good wasn't it?

Roxy

Of course it was. You had me to help you write it.

Vincent

So why do we have to revisit it?

Roxy

Because now Flow Posse now you have the tools to put it to work for you. It's what gets you moving towards your end results.

Vincent

So what do we have to add to that previous chapter?

Creating creative structure in consciousness

Roxy

Now that's a good question, even if it took you long enough to get there.

(Sigh)

Humans!

So, Flow Posse, now you have your choices, you need to create a creative structure in your consciousness that compels those choices to resolve towards your end result.

And what do you need to create that structure? You already have the end results from your choices. The other part of structure that you need, is current reality.

When you have both, then you have a structure in consciousness. And that structure will provide you with the wisdom – the ideas, insights, next steps – that you need to move towards your end result.

> **Key insight:**
> When you combine the end results from your choice with the current reality and hold both in your consciousness, you have a structure that will provide you with the ideas, insights, and next steps to move forward towards your end results.

Vincent

So how do you define current reality?

Roxy

It's very simple. It's where you are now with respect to your choice.

Vincent

You make it sound so simple.

Roxy

Of course I make it simple. Super-simple. I'm exceptionally good at that. You humans need it.

Vincent

You're just big-noting yourself again. We are capable of understanding this at a deeper level.

Roxy

I know that. It seems I have to remind you – again, I am not stupid. Far from it. Do I need to remind you every time that I wrote ...

But I don't have time for that today.

Flow Posse, I know most of you can understand it at a deeper level. It has to be simple, though, so you can apply it.

Let's do an example. Let's look at one of your choices, Vincent. You have a choice about creating your own brand of books. Imaginatively create a circle of what the end result looks like, jump in and tell me what's you pick up.

Vincent

When I tune into that, I see a shelf full of books. I wrote some ...

Roxy

We wrote some. Please.

Vincent

Sorry Roxy. We wrote some, other people wrote others, I might even have written books with another muse. Is that OK?

Roxy

I have no idea why you would want to write with another muse but I suppose it's just because you're human; or perhaps you want to work in another genre. I work with other authors, why shouldn't you work with other muses? It's not cheatin', like they sing about in country music. It's just work.

And is there anything else in that end result?

Vincent

The series of books have a theme. Right now, I feel it's Magic and Flow.

Roxy

Now that's a theme that you humans need. Very good, VG.

And what else is there in the vision? Where's that bookshelf?

Vincent

It's in a bookshop. Isn't that obvious?

Roxy

Not at all. So many of you humans love to write books but never get them reviewed or published let alone read by other people. It could just be that your book is a manuscript sitting on a shelf at home gathering dust. Have you done that?

Vincent

Well yes. My first book was just plain terrible ...

Roxy

True. That's exactly what the poor fellow you paid to review it said.

Vincent

... and the second one that I wrote without a muse never got completed.

Roxy

I rest my case. So why are you trying again?

Vincent

I'd always seen books in my HeartVision but never had one that felt true to work on. Then intuition gave me this and I just knew that I had to write it. It was that simple. And when I started, I rediscovered how much I loved writing. And then you joined me.

Roxy

So I did, and even now, you don't fully appreciate how lucky you are, if I say so myself.

So having those books on display in a bookshop is a powerful end result. Especially if some of those are yours and especially if those first two books you wrote were never close to good enough to be published.

And would there be anything else in that end result?

Vincent

It feels like the bookshop is part of a chain.

Roxy

Now that's very interesting, isn't it? So there is a wide demand for them?

Vincent

Well, yes.

Roxy

And I would not have chosen to work with you if your vision – at least for yourself – had been any smaller.

So Vincent, create a new circle that's the current reality of this choice, and jump into that one.

Vincent

Well, I only have this book and it's only partly done.

Roxy

And what else is there in your current reality?

Vincent

I'm keeping an eye open among my clients, students and network for people working on books with a magic and flow theme.

Roxy

Very good. And what else is there in your current reality?

Vincent

Well, it feels like this choice is very big. Overwhelming. How long will it take me to create all that? Even getting this book complete, published, and promoted feels like a long way off.

Roxy

Please take note, Flow Posse. This is interesting. This is important. Current reality is never just about what's going on in the physical world. It's also about what thoughts and feelings are coming up for you; and what parts of your shadow are triggered as well. Very often your shadow will agree that the vision is indeed well worth having; BUT as a first step, it needs to address all those beliefs that hold you back.

Let's take one of your beliefs, Vincent. You believe you're insignificant, that people won't listen to you.
So, if you allow that belief to have power in your consciousness, then the first thing you have to do is something that does indeed make you more significant. The problem with this belief is that it comes from a place where you don't know what you have to do to be significant. Worse, you don't realize that you don't know. So you do something you think will make yourself more significant. You take a training course, for example in public speaking. And are you more significant when you're done? You have some skills in speaking in front of people but what about the message? Where's the audience going to come from? The belief kicks in again. Certainly, you're better than you

were. You've experienced some valuable growth, but you're still not significant. And although you do more and more to fulfil the belief but it's never enough.

In the meantime, you're making zero direct progress towards your vision.

> **Key insights:**
> Your current reality with respect to a choice comprises both the physical reality (what you've created so far, challenges and risks) and also your psychological current reality – what beliefs are being triggered, what unconscious agendas are informing you, and how you may be sabotaging yourself.

Now, we could spend a lot more time on Vincent's shadow, his limiting beliefs, assumptions and definitions, but that's for another book.

Vincent

We're doing a book about my shadow? All my beliefs faults, failings, and stuff-ups?

Roxy

A book about all your beliefs, faults, failings, and stuff-ups? More like a trilogy at least. In four parts. And the rest. After all, you do need to fill those bookshelves you saw in the stores. I rather think those books would sell well. I'm looking forward to working on it, aren't you?

And don't even think about answering that question.

Very good, though, Vincent. What you have given is your end result. Now, you have given us your current reality. And you have been honest about it. You've looked for the truth – especially about where you're at. There's been no denial of what's going on in the physical or the shadow. We only cut that part a little short because this book isn't the place for a full in-depth exposé of all your sabotage.

So when you have current reality and an end result, what does that create?

Creative Tension

Vincent

Creative tension.

Roxy

Very good.

Yes, Flow Posse, when we have an intuitive vision of our end result and a true and insightful view of all aspects of our current reality, then we have Creative Tension. It's a force in consciousness that is set to resolve itself in the direction of the end result.

You can picture it this way. Pick up a rubber band. If you hold one end, it's like having only an end result. If you hold the other end, it's like having only current reality. If you hold both ends and stretch it, then you have tension, which will tend to resolve to the end you hold onto.

> **Key insight:**
> When you hold an end result and your current reality in your consciousness, you have creative tension that will try to resolve in the direction of the end result.

You do need the truth – an accurate insight into current reality just as much as you need the truth about where you're going. Without an accurate current reality you'll be led in the wrong direction. Remember the lady who booked that flight from Birmingham Alabama to Las Vegas? Imagine if she'd asked the pilot on that flight 'How do you get from Birmingham to Las Vegas?' He probably would have said 'Fly slightly north of west for about four hours'. Then imagine her getting a private plane from Birmingham UK and saying to the pilot, "We're going to Vegas. Fly slightly north of west for about four hours'. The pilot would refuse to take off. Four hours slightly north of west from Birmingham UK is in the middle of the Atlantic Ocean.

In other words, an inaccurate current reality will compel an action in the wrong direction.

And if you don't acknowledge current reality at all, if you just dream of your end result, you will create no tension and compel no action.

Now this is important, it doesn't matter how you get to your end result. Just stay with the intention of making your way from current reality towards the end result and you will get guidance from intuition about how to get there. Your journey will be like a river, sometimes direct; and, sometimes it will follow the path of least resistance and meander and wind as it finds the easiest way to get to your end result.

OK so far?

Vincent

Yes. So how exactly does creative tension work to get to the end result?

Roxy

It creates a creative structure in consciousness. In your consciousness, to be sure. But your consciousness is connected to the consciousness of the universe, so it is there too. And this creative structure is compelled to resolve in favor of your end result. And so consciousness creates for you intuitive ideas, insights and promptings that will lead you on the path of least resistance towards the end result. It also creates favorable circumstances – opportunities, synchronicities, coincidences as it works through the consciousness of people who can help you so that they are led to align with you and your end results. And not only the consciousness of other people but the consciousness of the universe. This is the magic. This is the flow.

> **Key insight:**
> When you hold your creative structure in your consciousness, you will receive ideas, insights promptings opportunities, coincidences and synchronicities which lead you on the path of least resistance towards your end results.

Vincent

Wow. I love how clearly you expressed that.

Roxy

Thank you Vincent. That felt like it came from a place even higher than me.

So tell me, Vincent, creative tension is a force in consciousness but can you feel it?

Vincent

Yes you can. Sometimes it's exciting and delightful when it's resolving towards your end result – like a piece of writing or a painting or a website all coming together.

Often, it's uncomfortable though. You feel things should be moving faster and they don't.

Roxy

So what happens then?

Vincent

Now when that happens, your shadow steps in and offers you ways out of that discomfort. Trouble is, those are the ways you sabotage yourself. They're temptations. We call it resolving the tension dysfunctionality.

You might be tempted to just give up. You advertise a service, perhaps run a webinar to promote it, perhaps make many sales calls and nobody buys.

Roxy

Like the webinars you ran a couple of years ago, Vincent?

Vincent

Do you have to remind me? That was painful and the memory still is.

Roxy

Yes Vincent. And pain is a challenge and, so, an opportunity for growth. It's good for you. I'll look forward to seeing what you create next. So what would you usually do next?

Vincent

In the past, I'd have come to the conclusion that my offering was defective or that I'd never be good enough at sales to be successful with it or both. And just give up.

Roxy

And, in the past, you've done that, haven't you, Vincent?

Vincent

Yes. And I know the beliefs behind it and how to deal with them. As you'd say, there's a book in that.

Roxy

Not a book, a trilogy.

But how else can you sabotage creative tension.

Vincent

If you have an action to take, you might be tempted into inessential activity. House cleaning is very common because it feels like you're clearing the space so you can take action – and then, suddenly, you find you've run out of time to take that action.

Roxy

I wouldn't accuse you publicly of being untidy; but, sometimes, I think you could use that one. What else?

Vincent

Sometimes intuition says do nothing. We call that hanging with the tension. But we are so conditioned to taking action to create that we have to be doing something. Doing nothing and hanging out with that creative tension is uncomfortable.

Roxy

Why might that be?

Vincent

Have you ever had a fellow muse say to you 'Look busy, the boss is coming'? So you have to find something to do to make it look like you're working?

Roxy

Why would we want to do that? We just work. Why do you humans have to make life so complicated? It's short enough as it is.

Vincent

Let's just say it's because we're humans.

So we find something to do, to resolve that tension and relieve the discomfort. Often, that is by doing what we know we know is possible and easy rather than what is required to take us to our end result. As a result, we end up with an outcome that's a pale shadow of what our heart envisaged. For example, we might see a fast red sports car in our vision but we end up getting a small yellow eco-hatchback.

Roxy

What could possibly be wrong with that? It's better for the planet, better for the spine, hips and knees, and perfect for the stop-start traffic you find yourselves in all the time. Also, the car may be modest but the modern sound systems are brilliant.

Vincent

You're absolutely right Roxy. And yet, if we get a red sports car in our HeartVision, then that's what is true for us to choose.

Nevertheless, we often end up resolving the tension by settling for a lesser result that was in our HeartVision; and then find justification for why we settled.

Our shadows and our greatness are equally creative; and we have to be vigilant to keep our focus on our vision and not on resolving tension dysfunctionally. After all, our shadow believes it's keeping us safe – and doesn't see that it's just following the beliefs, assumptions and definitions laid down in childhood. And that's a powerful force.

> **Key insight:**
> As you move towards your end results, your shadow continually tries to disrupt your progress with resistance and distractions and the temptation to settle for something less than the end result that you desire.

Roxy

Very good VG.

Now, can you summarize this chapter?

Summary

Vincent

We need to use a creative structure to compel the creation of the end results of our choices. The choice gives us the end result; and, to complete the structure, we need to get the truth about our current reality – both the physical and the psychological – the beliefs, definitions and assumptions that lurk in our shadow.

From this, we get creative tension, a force in consciousness that gives us insights and promptings; and also works with others and the universe to create the opportunities, synchronicities and coincidences we need to create our end results.

And, because creative tension is often uncomfortable, we have to stay vigilant so that we're not tempted by our shadow into resolving that tension in a dysfunctional way.

Roxy

Very good, Vincent. We have alignment and structure. What else do we need?

Vincent

Energy.

Roxy

Exactly. We'll work on that next.

Chapter 20

Energy

How we get help from the universe

Vincent

So, Roxy, what do we have to do, if anything – to start the creative tension resolving towards our end results?

Roxy

That's an excellent question to start the day.

The answer is that you've completed the first two steps. You've created the choice, which is alignment and created a creative structure by getting to the truth about your current reality. This creates creative tension, that force in consciousness that is poised to resolve in favor of your end result. Now you have to put energy in to kick-start that resolution.

Vincent

And how do we do that?

> **Key insight:**
> For your choice to resolve towards your end result, you have to put energy in.

Using daily choices to direct your consciousness

Roxy

This is important. Flow Posse, listen up!

The first step in adding energy into our choices is to go through them and tune in to them each day, every day.

Now it's not just a matter of pulling out your phone, while you're on your way to work, scrolling through your list, scanning them like a Tibetan prayer wheel and you're all done. You need to do more than just read through them. Ask yourselves, how much energy is in that? You're giving your subconscious the message that your choices don't really matter to you.

What you need to do is to find a quiet place and time where you'll be undisturbed for around ten minutes. Then read each choice, come into innosense, create a circle defined as the end result of that choice, step in and feel yourself in it. Really feel the emotion in that end result. Then move on to the next one. Allow around a minute for each choice.

Simple isn't it? What could be so hard about that?

Vincent

Finding ten minutes doesn't sound hard but we humans are very time pressured. Our days seem to be scripted from the moment we get up. Some of us have children to look after and some of us have to get to work.

Roxy

'But you humans are very time pressured'. But-heads!

Tell me, Vincent, how could you make the time if you have children or have to get to work?

Vincent

I guess that if the children are little, you could do choices at nap time. Or perhaps after the children have gone off to school or off to bed.

If you go to a job every day, perhaps find that ten minutes on the way home or on the way to work or during a break. And it's important to set aside the time on your days off too when you have a different routine.

Roxy

Very good VG, and I'm sure the Flow Posse can get just as creative whatever challenge they face.

Because, let's be very clear, if you humans want to live from magic and flow, that's what it takes. You have 1440 minutes in a day, and only need ten to do your choices – how hard could that be?

Humans!

What do you do Vincent?

Vincent

I used to do them last thing at night. It was always a quiet time for me. But when I started working on this book, I'd be staying up later and started to doze off. So I switched to mornings after my yoga.

Roxy

And you do that every day?

Vincent

There are some days when I'm out of my routine. I have to be up super-early. Perhaps I need to be on a morning flight. On those days, I'm careful to make the time later in the day, so that the choices do get done.

Roxy

And do you?

Vincent

> The hardest days are when I'm totally out of my routine with a super-early start and one thing after another after another until late at night. I have very few days like that but that makes it harder to deal with. There were a couple of times that happened; I fell asleep doing them at the end of the day.

Roxy

> Humans! And with the benefit of hindsight, could you have found a way, a time to do them earlier on that day?

Vincent

> Yes. The last couple of times I've had full-on days, I've found a way to do them where I could not fall asleep before they were done – like standing up.

Roxy

> Well, at least you're honest – most of the time.
>
> I can't repeat this enough. The first step in living from magic and flow is to do your choices each and every day. So, Flow Posse, it's over to each of you to find a time in your day when can I fit your choices into your routine, where you can set that ten to fifteen minutes aside. First thing in the morning, last thing at night, somewhere in between. Your choice. Choose it!
>
> Some of you will not get out of bed till the choices are done. Others have to deal with a baby, first thing in the morning, and will have to find another time. If your routine varies over the week, or you work shifts, then you'll need to identify when to do choices depending on what's on for that day. But it's only ten to fifteen minutes. You can always find a time. Even if you have to do them before you go to bed – standing up, as Vincent says, so you don't doze off.
>
> It's so important that you put the power in your choices, in your vision, in this way. Because if you don't you'll end up sabotaging yourself and re-creating everything you don't want.
>
> And would you have any other tips, Vincent?

Vincent

Yes, you can make an audio recording of your choices and use that when you go through them. What's important is that you get yourself into innosense and get into the embodied feeling and emotion of the end result.

Roxy

And you do that?

Vincent

Yes.

Roxy

So, the first way to put energy in is to do your choices daily.

And it's the most important way. It's non-negotiable. If there is only one way you put energy into your choices, this is it.

> **Key insight:**
> The first step in living from magic and flow is to do your choices each and every day. It's a non-negotiable daily discipline.
> You can read them or make your own audio recording (as Vincent does). The process should take around ten minutes.

Take the obvious action

What's the next way?

Vincent

Take action.

Roxy

Not quite. You're missing something. What's obvious about what you've missed about taking action?

Vincent

I'm tired. Give me a clue.

Roxy

Sometimes, I wish I was physical, at least enough to slap you about the face to wake you up.

With love. Tough love.

The answer is so obvious; I'll wager half the Flow Posse are screaming it at you already.

However, as you're only a human, I'll give you a clue. Come back to the kayaking metaphor. That should help.

Vincent

That's it? That's the clue?

Roxy

What more do you need?

Humans!

Talk it through.

Vincent

Well in the metaphor, it's getting in the kayak and paddling out into the current. That's obvious.

Roxy

What's obvious about the action you took?

Vincent

Well, you get in the current and you head off downstream.

Roxy

Don't be so smug. Why do I have to spoon-feed you tonight? Why can't you just translate back from the metaphor to the original question?

Vincent

Ahhh. It's taking the obvious aligned action.

Roxy

And you complain about me making you work. How much did you make me do just then?

Tell me, how can you be sure that the action is aligned?

Vincent

Now I'm onto it. It has to come from intuition. Not from a plan – although if you do have a plan, you'll often get the same answer both ways.

Roxy

This is like getting blood out of a stone. Did I ever tell you, I helped a Persian magus in the way distant past get blood from a stone and, I promise you, that was easier.

(sigh)

So what tools can our Flow Posse use to be sure they are getting the obvious aligned action?

Using vision – current reality – bridge circles to get the next action step

Vincent

The classic go-to-tool is the vision – current-reality-bridge technique, which uses circles.

The first circle is the end result or vision. You go into innosense, define the circle as the end result and feel it powerfully, getting a sense of what it looks like and the energy and emotion there.

Then you step out of that, create a second circle, which is the current reality of the choice and get a sense of what that looks like and also how your shadow – your limiting beliefs or definitions – are at work to sabotage you.

Getting into the Flow

Copyright - Public Domain – from *https://pxhere.com/en/photo/1257923*

Finally, you come out of that circle. You imagine a bridge.

Roxy

What sort of bridge, Vincent? The Golden Gate bridge? The Rialto in Venice? Tower Bridge in London? A suspension footbridge high in the mountains?

Is it over a large wide river? A small dried up creek? A bridge over troubled waters? Between islands? Across a mountain valley?

Vincent

Flow Posse, you can make the bridge and the landscape whatever works for you – but don't make it a distraction. It's just a tool. That's why I prefer to keep it simple – a small river and a plank bridge, like the photo.

In your imagination, you move the current reality circle over to the far side. You bring up the end result circle on the near side. You drop back into innosense and step into that end result circle. Feel the emotion. Get a powerful sense of what it's like to be in the end result. In this place of being in the end result, you have an intuitive knowing of how you got here.

So now, look back at the current reality and ask intuitively, 'what's the next obvious step I took to move forward from there?' And remember to take the very first thing that comes to mind before you have time to think about it.

> **Key insight:**
> To create your end results, you need to take obvious aligned action that comes from intuition.
> This is done by first using a circle to tune into the end result or vision; then stepping out of that circle and into a second circle to tune into your current reality; then stepping out of that circle, moving it to the far side of some water, bringing back the vision circle and stepping in; and from that place, asking intuitively what the next obvious step is.

Other tools for getting aligned action

Roxy

At last. You got there.

So, Flow Posse, what's really important is that when you have been through all of your choices and tuned in to the end results, you then choose two of them and get your bridges, your next steps.

Yes, I know you use an imaginary bridge to get the next step and you also call that next step a bridge. Confused? The bridge you imagine is a metaphor. What that metaphor corresponds to in the real world is the action step bridge.

And what next Vincent?

Vincent

You take that action as soon as possible.

Roxy

> Very good VG.

Spirit Guidance

> Now, are there any other tools for getting aligned action?

Vincent

> Well sometimes, an aligned action will become obvious just while you're in the circle of the end result.
>
> Sometimes, you'll use a circle to get an answer to a question you have and an action will drop in from that.
>
> And finally, there is Spirit Guidance for when you want more detailed information. You don't need to believe in spirit guides to use the process – you can treat is as a purely imaginative process or you can believe you are connecting in some way with spirit. Your choice. In this process, you use a guided meditation to connect with a spirit guide, they tell you what you need to know, and you journal it. You can get that as my 'Thank you' gift to you when you sign up to stay connected with me on my website.
>
> There's a link to that process below and also in Appendix 1 Exercises and resources ...
> https://vincentgmelling.com/gitf-symbols-and-beyond

> You want more? You always do.

Roxy

> I'm sure I could squeeze more out of you as surely as I was able to get that magus to get that blood from a stone. However, I don't want to overload our Flow Posse for now. The Vision / Current Reality / Bridge and the Spirit Guide are a great start.

Now please remind me, what you do when you've got the next action to take?

Vincent

You take that action as soon as possible. Ideally, straight after you've received it. It may not always be possible to take the action straight away. For example, you may need to wait for someone else to do something or a delivery to come. That's OK - just take the action as soon as you can

Roxy

I never thought we'd get here. That's all you have to do isn't it.

Sometimes, you'll get the logical next step from the last action you took, like following a plan. Sometimes, you'll get a do nothing or do some gardening or go for a walk. Those do not appear to be moving forward. However, when you take that action, you find it's usually to allow you to get to a place where the next action can just drop in and it may indeed be different from whatever your logical mind expected. Sometimes, you'll just get an action straight away from the bridge circle that feels like a change of course, very left field.

Whatever it is, yes, you're right; take that action as soon as you can.

> **Key insight:**
> Spirit guidance is a way to get a deeper insight into a choice, into the actions it requires and also to help you with day-to-day problems in any area of life.

Adding in subtle energy

Roxy

So now, Flow Posse,

You have a structures in your consciousness set up to resolve in favor of the end results of your choices.

You have put energy in to maintain those structures and kick-start that resolution by getting and auctioning bridges.

A final way to put energy into a structure to kick-start the resolution is to use subtle energy.

So, Vincent, please start by telling me, what types of subtle energy are there?

Vincent

There's a ton of them. Kundalini energy, Prana, Ojas, Chi. Reiki, Huna, Red Bull, and that's just some of the better known examples. You can imaginatively pull subtle energy from nature, the earth, plants, the sky and the heavens.

Just don't talk subtle energy to a physicist.
They will pretend not to understand you.

Then they'll be the first to get acupuncture if they've hurt their back. Just don't ask them about how it works.

Roxy

Very good, VG. Now the secret is that some of these energies are frequencies that flow mainly in the body. Some of them are most valuable to heal the body and you manipulate them in healing modalities – the prana, reiki and chi. Like your acupuncturist sister-in-law.

Vincent

My mother says that thanks to acupuncture, she keeps very healthy. Otherwise my sister-in law will come and stick needles in her.

Roxy

She's a very wise woman, your mother.

Yes. So some energies are healing for the body, the mind, and the spirit.

However, there is another class of energy that is of a higher frequency and altogether more powerful. And you can put them to work to help create your end results. In this class there are Kundalini energy, sex energy, and energy you pull from nature. That's the energy of creation itself. It's energy at the frequency of consciousness – so you can add it to the structure you've created in consciousness to build up its power. The specific techniques include energy pulls, deep breathwork and conscious transmutation of sexual energy for example, in a tantric or a Chaos Magick ritual. You just set the intention for the use of the energy at the outset and keep coming back to it. The sexual energy is so strong because it has the power to open a portal to allow a soul to come through from the astral and into a physical being – whether or not that actually happens, or is possible in the sex act. As tantric lovemaking often lasts hours, just imagine how much energy you can infuse into your conscious structure this way.

All this energy increases the creative tension like stretching a rubber band and as you do that, the force in consciousness that compels resolution increases and increase until the magic has to start dropping in. The coincidences, opportunities, synchronicities, perfect timing and what you humans call just being lucky.

Key insight:
You can use intention to add subtle energies from any energetic practice(s) you know to the structures in consciousness that you create from your choices.

What happens when you keep stretching a rubber band, Vincent?

Vincent
When you stretch it far enough, it breaks.

Roxy

And there's where the metaphor breaks down. Literally. And we need to consider one more metaphor for creative tension. Because you can keep adding energy and tension to the structure in consciousness and it will never break.

What we can learn from crystallization

The system in consciousness that you call creative tension is also like a solution of Epsom salts. You dissolve some in hot water.

Vincent

This is a simple experiment folks. Please please PLEASE do it in a container that will take boiling-hot water. Please don't use a glass or anything else that might break with the heat and that's dangerous. Don't use a bathtub. The experiment will still work in a bathtub it will take longer and you'll need sacks of Epsom salts. Probably the easiest way if you want to do it is to buy a crystal kit from the science section of a toy store.

Roxy

Very good.

What happens when you keep adding Epsom salts till you can't dissolve any more?

Vincent

That's called a saturated solution. It's ready to crystallize.

Roxy

And why do we use hot water?

Vincent

Because you can dissolve more Epsom salts in hot water than in cold. It's the same for most if not all salts.

Roxy

So what happens when we create a saturated solution of Epsom salts in hot water; then cool it? For example, in the refrigerator?

Vincent

The Epsom salts crystallize out. And the crystals are beautiful. You can make them even prettier by adding some food coloring before you put them in the fridge.

Roxy

And that's exactly how creative tension works too. You keep adding energy until it can't help but crystallize out beautifully. And what's the difference between the Epsom salts we started with and the beautiful crystals we end up with?

Vincent

Crystals have a highly ordered microscopic structure. The molecules are not ordered randomly.

Roxy

You had to Google that didn't you?

Vincent

Only because I needed the precise wording.

Roxy

And how does that relate to the flow?

Vincent

When the system in consciousness has enough tension, like when the water has enough Epsom salts dissolved in it – it will resolve in a very ordered way back into physicality. And we'll see this as the synchronicities, opportunities, and perfect timing of the flow. And in my experience perfect creative flow like when I'm writing and everything about it just seems to fall into place perfectly. The exact words in the exact order.

Roxy

Very good, VG. I almost said perfect but I can't let you get carried away.

So in the metaphor, we put the crystals in the refrigerator to cool. What's the real world equivalent?

Vincent

Keep taking the actions that arise from your bridges and adding subtle energy.

Roxy

You're on the ball today. Remember, the idea is not to move smoothly along a project plan to create what you want. There's no reason not to have a plan and planning from intuition will often surface necessary actions. Your main task is to keep adding energy and keep following your intuition, taking the actions that come from it, until you've added so much energy, the end result has to crystallize out from consciousness. And why keep taking action even when you think you've done enough?

Vincent

Two reasons.

Obviously, you can't see how much more energy the creative tension system needs.

And then, in the metaphor, there's a quirk that you wouldn't expect. When you cool a saturated solution by twenty degrees, then it has more Epsom salts dissolved in it than you'd be able to dissolve if you started out with water at that temperature. Yet it won't crystallize. That is called a super-saturated solution.

The solution won't necessarily crystallize straight away, just because you cool it.

Some solutions require something to kick-start the crystallization. In chemistry, we add a seed crystal. and then the whole solution will crystallize; and if it's super-saturated, it will be very fast.

Roxy

Very good, VG. So as you keep taking action, you're not just adding more energy, you're also creating the equivalent of little seed crystals so that as soon as the creative tension system is ready, it will crystallize out.

Now when you went to Uluru, that's how it happened. Small actions, nothing happening, COVID lockdowns. And then the whole end result crystallized out, each step in quick succession. Lockdowns ended, flights booked, you got into the Uluru National Park while it was open, you were at the meditation, opportunities came up. That's what it feels like in the physical world.

> **Key insight:**
> Often, the resolution of a choice is not linear. You keep taking action and adding other forms of energy; and you may not see immediate results. Then with more energy, the structure reaches a tipping point and your results unfold quickly like a saturated solution crystallizing.

Success breeds Success – so celebrate!

Roxy

And there is one final way to add energy.

Have you ever heard the saying "Success breeds success".

Vincent

When I worked in recruitment all those years ago, the big boss used to quote it all the time.

Roxy

He must have been a very wise big boss.

Vincent

He was.

Actually, he wasn't very big though. He was quite a short boss.

But yes, very wise, as you say.

Roxy

That's because it's super-important to acknowledge your success. When you do that you're giving your consciousness and your light team a number of powerful messages. That you are on track. That you are a masterful creator. That you can do this! That you're learning and growing and ready to create whatever's next and it will better than anything that has gone before.

Vincent

That's pretty obvious isn't it.

Roxy

Of course.

But you'd be surprised how many of you humans refuse to do it.

You humans say, 'I'm just doing my job'.

Or somehow you feel that your success is not worth celebrating – too small, not worth celebrating, not impressive enough.

Vincent, you refuse to do it a lot don't you?

Vincent

I used to. These days, I make a practice of acknowledging what I create.

Roxy

Very good, VG. You have to acknowledge every successful step before you move on. You don't have to spend a lot of money or do anything special. A happy dance will more than suffice. But you must acknowledge yourself in some way.

Why?

Because it builds a snowball effect.

It doesn't seem much to start out with but it builds and builds and builds your energy, confidence and capabilities and, before you know it, you're taking huge leaps forward and your life has real momentum.

> **Key insight:**
> Acknowledging and celebrating success is critical to building your capacity to create.

Very good, VG

We're at the end of another chapter so we'll stop, take a break and celebrate now.

Summary

Vincent

Thanks Roxy. What about the usual summary?

Roxy

Why ask me? Of course you have to do the summary first.

Vincent

Once you have a structure and it's aligned, you have to put energy in. The first and most important step is to establish a daily choices practice. That includes getting bridges. The next steps towards your end results; and taking those actions, you can add additional energy through transmuting subtle energy. And, finally, acknowledge and celebrate your successes as you create them. This helps your creativity and energy gathers momentum, like a snowball.

Roxy

Now you have completed the chapter and you can do your happy dance. All of you Flow Posse. Get creative, find a way to acknowledge yourselves.

Part 6

Living in Flow

Chapter 21

Engaging the flow

Roxy

So, Flow Posse, we have shown you how to create alignment, create structure and tension; and add energy.

Vincent, would you tell the Flow Posse what happens next?

Vincent

Well, creating the alignment structure and energy sets you up to move forward. You know where the flow is and you know just what you need do to launch yourself into it.

It's like with a kayak; you've found your river, there's water in it. you know where you're going, you just have to paddle out and get into the current,

Roxy

So how do you take this work out into your daily life?

Daily choices

Vincent

As I just said in the last chapter, do your choices every day, get bridges and take action.

Roxy

That's the most important thing. Action that next step.

You may just get one action. You may get a whole sequence of actions.

Getting into the Flow

What's important is that you take that first action and move forward. Then tune in again.

Sometimes that first action is exactly what was in the plan. Sometimes, intuition gives you something unexpected.

But, always, take the next step.

Take the next step

Vincent

Why wouldn't you?

Roxy

Why wouldn't I? Why me? It's you humans that don't.

Perhaps because it sounds too much like hard work?
Because you don't want to call that person?
Because you don't want to post what you need to post on social media because you'll be judged?

Because you need to feed the cat or walk the dog?
You humans are soooo good at coming up with excuses for not taking action.

This next one is interesting... You humans say
'I don't want to take action because the next step that's come to me from a bridge seems to make no sense because it's not moving me forward. Like take a bath or do the gardening or, even, sometimes, walk the dog.'

Don't you humans realize that that's when the best ideas drop in? When you're working hard and concentrating and focusing, you shut down the openness you have when you're more relaxed.

And all of those reasons for not taking action are just thoughts and feelings created by your dysfunctional belief systems?

Do you get that?

Vincent

Yes

Roxy

And so whenever you won't take the action you've been given, you give your consciousness a powerful message about where the power is.

And it's not in your greatness, not in what you truly desire. It's in your ego, your shadow, your core wounding.

Got it?

Vincent

Yes

Roxy

Not taking action is like sitting in a backwater going nowhere.

> **Key insight:**
> The first key to Living in the Flow is to do your choices daily and take the actions that come from that practice.

Getting into the Flow

Figure 9: Vincent G. Melling - Rapids on the Yarra River - . 7 March 2021

Living in the flow – running the rapids

Roxy

So, tell me, Vincent, how does a kayaking trip start?

Vincent

When everybody has their boats in the water, we set off. We get into the current. But the launching places are often on fairly flat water where the current is not strong and you have to paddle to keep up. That's OK.

Then the leader gets you all to pull over to the bank. Because up ahead is the first rapid of the day – woo hoo!

Rapids are a place where there's a drop in the riverbed and it's significantly lower on the far side. There are usually rocks that form like a dam that holds most of the water back and a narrow channel where the river rushes through at speed. Sometimes there is more than one channel and one is easier than the others. Perhaps the river is shallow and that one channel is where the water is deeper. Perhaps the river is fuller and it's the gentler, safer channel.

There is usually a clean clear way through the rapids. The way the main flow of the river goes. And you need to be in that flow and well aligned. Otherwise, you could be swept into the shallows or pinned or wedged against a rock. The guides will tell you the best way through – follow the left or the right – aim just to the left of that rock, make a sharp turn at this point and so on, They'll give you directions and you focus and trust that guidance implicitly. Or you lose focus and the river will find you out.

And when you do get stuck, the water flows with such force in the rapids, there are ways to use it to help you get unstuck.

Rapids are fun. Exciting. Exhilarating.

Roxy

So, Vincent, let's apply that back to living in the flow.

At first you're aligned and taking step after step and in a way it feels like how you've always worked.

And then you come to the rapids and it looks like your way forward is blocked, doesn't it?

Vincent

It does from a distance. But as you get closer – often right up to them you can see where the water flows through.

Roxy

That's interesting. Why do you think that is?

Vincent

Because the water has to make its way downstream.

Roxy

Why?

Vincent

Well that's a dumb question.

Why does water flow downhill? It just does. It's very good at finding ways to do it.

Roxy

(sigh)

I feel like this is déjà vu. I don't ask dumb questions. I ask profound metaphysical questions designed to make you go deeper past all those mental shortcuts all you humans have and all I get back is attitude. Now tell me, why does that water flow downstream?

Vincent

Because that's its essential nature? It takes a serious dam to stop it flowing. And it's basic physics. Water's a fluid. If there's a lower place it can get to, it will go there.

Roxy

And you said water is very good at finding its way downhill.

Vincent

I did.

Roxy

So does that mean that water is pretty smart? That it's trained hard to recognize all the situations it might get into and still be able to find a way downhill?

Vincent

No it doesn't. I didn't say water was smart or well-trained. Flowing downhill is just what it does naturally.

Roxy

That's a very good insight VG. So how does that translate to when you're in the flow of life?

Vincent

Well, I guess it's the same. You've created a structure and put energy in and now that the energy has to follow the structure.

It will find a way through and take you with it. You'll come to places you appear to be blocked but as you get up close, that's where the fun shows up; that's. It's where the coincidences, synchronicities, chance meetings and phone calls happen out of the blue. It's where the magic happens. It's where everything starts coming together, one thing after another and it seems so quick and so exciting.

> **Key insight:**
> Sometimes, the way ahead appears blocked, like rapids on a river. But when you get up close, you'll see there is a way through and that's where the magic is most likely to show up.

Roxy

Very good, VG.

What about the guides that lead the kayaking trip?

Vincent

I guess that's a metaphor for your intuition or your spirit guides are telling you to position yourself right so that you can make the most of the flow and not get stuck.

Roxy

Very good, VG. Very good. It took you long enough, though, didn't it?

Humans!

And what about getting stuck? Like against the side of a rock? Or in a shallow part of the rapids?

Vincent

It will feel like you're stuck but with a little effort, you can free yourself just enough for the flow of the river to lift the kayak and carry you forwards.

Roxy

So how would that translate to living in the flow?

Vincent

OMG almost word for word, just changing the word 'river' to 'energy'.

It's simple. Sometimes, it feels like you're stuck with a choice. You can be wondering why you're not making progress. But when you apply a process for looking at unwanted results, like the Sabotage Spotlight process, you can very quickly see what's holding you up and take action to move past it and back into the flow.

Roxy

Very good, VG

Dirty great rapids

Roxy

So what about when you've done this easy trip once or twice or maybe even several times over.

Vincent

Well, you'll want to go further afield. Find next-level rivers with bigger and badder rapids that are more fun to do.

Roxy

And what if you don't have a guide to show you through those rapids.

Vincent

You'll want to pull out of the main current and over to the bank and check them out first. It's just prudent. You can preview the rapids, see what's out there. Plot your course and head off, or possibly even carry the boat around them if it doesn't look safe. But it's not okay to kind of see the rapids and give up.

That's why a guide is so valuable; and the guide is a metaphor for a coach in the real world.

Roxy

Now, Flow Posse, please be aware that there is a difference here between canoeing as a metaphor, and life. The bigger the life you lead, the more you grow, the bigger the rapids – the challenges – that are going to be thrown at you because you are capable of navigating them. You have built that capability. And now you're being led to grow through this next challenge. You have powerful tools to move through it including holding your end results, following your intuition, and working with your coach. Trust your tools and trust the process.

> **Key insight:**
> Rapids can be fun but they can also be dangerous. It's best to have a guide. If you don't then it's prudent to be prudent. Rapids are a metaphor for challenges; and as you grow as an intuitive creator, the challenges that confront you will become greater but you will have the capacity to handle them.

Enjoying the journey

Roxy

Tell me one of the lessons you learned as you were about an hour into the kayak trip.

Vincent

Oh what – when I noticed the trees.

Roxy

Humans!
You're sooo fast asleep so much of the time.

How could you not notice the trees in the first place?

Vincent

> I was so pleased to be on the water and I was focusing there.
>
> And then it hit me.
>
> This river had high ground on both sides and the slopes were covered in trees and it was breathtakingly beautiful.
>
> And the day was sunny, the sky was bright blue. It was really a stunning sight and I felt blessed being there, on the water.

Roxy

> What do you think the lesson is?

Vincent

> Life's not just about getting to our end results.
>
> And the ultimate end result of life is death anyway as you keep reminding me.

Roxy

> True and true.

Vincent

> So why fixate on the end results at the expense of missing out on the beauty of the journey – those beautiful outcomes you have access to along the way. Put the focus on the actions you need, to be sure. But hold a wide awareness, like the innosense meditation. That's where the magic drops in.

Roxy

> And from time to time stop to smell the roses.

Vincent

> Ah Roxy, that's a terrible mixed metaphor. There are roses all over suburban streets and parks but very rarely by the side of the river.

Roxy

I think the Flow Posse are smart enough to know exactly what I mean.

> **Key insight:**
> Enjoy the journey of life and take time to stop and smell the roses.

The mountain

So now, Vincent, tell me about the mountain.

Vincent

Well the mountain has happened to me a couple of times now.

You follow a bend in the river and there directly ahead, a little way away is a mountain.

Roxy

Very good, VG. And what does that mean.

Vincent

At first sight, it freaked me out. It triggered a nightmare that I was somehow going to follow the river and crash into that mountain. That the river was carrying me to my doom. Or at the very least come to a complete stop there with no way out. Only a way back.

Roxy

And did you?

Vincent

No. There was another bend before the mountain and the river went off in a completely different direction.

Roxy

So you freaked out about nothing.

Vincent

Yes.

Roxy

Humans! I can't say I'm surprised. Where did you think that river was going to go?

Up and over the mountain?

Vincent

Obviously not.

Roxy

Was it just going to come to a complete standstill in a lake?

Vincent

Sometimes that happens – but I knew not on this stretch of the river.

Roxy

Or was the river just going to go around the mountain.

Vincent

Well, it could but that's how it is with rivers. One minute they're going one way and the next they are going in the opposite direction. It didn't go around the mountain, it went in a completely different direction. Following the path of least resistance I guess.

Roxy

And how does that translate to real life in the flow?

Vincent

Well in real life we often see major obstacles ahead.

Roxy

And you make up stories that you can't get around them, don't you?

Vincent

Well, yes.

Roxy

And stress about them and make plans.

When often enough they're not in your way at all. It's just an illusion you buy into. They just look like it while you're on a particular direction; then you turn and they're no longer in front of you. You can ignore them.

That's the structure you create, and the way the flow takes you through it.

There's no need to freak out whenever you see an obstacle. Just trust the flow to help you past it.

But I guess freaking out is only human.

Humans!

> **Key insight:**
> Often we see blocks in our path but they are mirages and there is always a way around them.

What wetsuits can teach us

Roxy

And what about wetsuits?

Vincent

Well, what about wetsuits?

OMG Don't tell me you've got a rubber fetish …

Roxy

Vincent! What are you thinking? I'm a spirit being with no sense of physical feeling. How could I?

You just have an overactive imagination!

(pause)

Oh, I'm sorry, perhaps I shouldn't have said that after all we've said about how important it is to be imaginative.

Vincent

Roxy, before you dig yourself in any deeper, it's just that when it's cold – which is another physical feeling you probably wouldn't understand, we wear wetsuits.

Roxy

Is it like making your own mobile comfort zone that goes everywhere with you?

Vincent

It is definitely comfortable especially when the weather is cool and the river is freezing. But that's not the only reason we wear them.

Roxy

And the other reason is that you like kinky?

Vincent

Sorry to disappoint you Roxy but no. It's beyond comfort. It's about staying healthy and safe. We humans could easily catch a nasty cold or even pneumonia so we need the right protection.

Roxy

Thank you, Vincent. Very good.

So the final lesson for this chapter is to identify, understand and manage your risks – which includes health and safety risk. All major projects have this. It's not to make you so fearful because the risk list is so long that you never take a step forward. It's just about having an awareness of the possibilities and how you're going to address them so you've cleared the way to move forward. For example, there's a risk of pneumonia – so you wear a wetsuit to stay warm. You might crash your car on the way to the canoeing trip; so you have insurance. You might fall out of the kayak and hit your head on a rock – so you wear a helmet. That might be because you weren't focused and alert – so don't go kayaking drunk or even hungover.

Vincent

There always seems to be someone hungover in the group.

Roxy

(sighs wearily)

Humans!

So, identifying, understanding, and managing risks is just prudence and care. It's not about finding excuses for not moving forward. Rather, you simply acknowledge current reality and the possibilities that could derail you; find a way to mitigate that risk – and you can do that intuitively with a circle; and then you find yourself free to move forward with confidence.

> **Key insight:**
> Be prudent – identify, understand and manage your risks.

Summary

Roxy

So, Vincent perhaps you can summarize.

Vincent

Just as kayaking down a river is not all smooth sailing and we have to deal with obstacles, both real and imaginary, along the way, so living in the flow is not always straightforward. We need

to trust our intuitive tools, and remember that the tension between our current reality and vision and is always working to resolve towards that vision and our job is to stay in that alignment, hang with that tension, not allow ourselves to back out, and enjoy the ride.

Roxy

Very good VG. We have given our Flow Posse a true treasure trove of information.

Being humans, they won't have retained much of it.

But, it's time to see if anything stuck.

Part 7

Conclusion and summary

Roxy

Let's recap what I've been telling you all in this book.

I'll make it a multiple choice test where the correct answers are drawn from the book;

1) Why would you want to get into the flow?
   a) So you win the lottery.
   b) Because kayaking is really great fun.
   c) Because the universe will help you with synchronicities, coincidences, and opportunities.
   d) So you can sit on the couch all day.
   e) Because I say so.
   f) All of the above.

2) Why does the universe help you when you're in the flow?
   a) Because the universe will always help you win the lottery if you focus long enough.
   b) Because the universe is full of unicorns (Yes, it is. Seriously.).
   c) Because it's creative, expanding and evolving and you're aligning with those forces.
   d) It feels like it's helping but it's sneakily setting you up to be pushed over a cliff.
   e) Because Miss Universe is a caring, sharing, wonderful human being.
   Just ask Donald Trump.

3) What did I say was wrong with sitting on the couch and visualizing millions of dollars coming to you?
   a) Nothing. I'm not judgmental. Although it is a total waste of time.
   b) You could be watching Netflix.
   c) You could be doing something useful.
   d) Couches are bad for your posture.

4) How did I say the universe started out?
   a) God made it in seven days.
   b) God actually got it done in six days with Sunday as his day off.
   c) It was made in China.
   d) It was proudly made in the USA.
   e) It started out with the Big Bang.

5) How much money did I say it cost to create the universe?
   a) About $10 trillion.
   b) The universe is one of many made by the fairy godmother of an inter-universal fairy tale heroine. It cost nothing but it will turn into a pumpkin at midnight, universe time.
   c) The universe didn't need money to create itself.
   d) 1000 Bitcoin (although Bitcoin used to be worth a lot more than they are now).

6) How do you create the greatest most beautiful version of yourself?
   a) Drink a couple of bottles of vodka, look in the mirror and tell yourself how amazing you are.
   b) Win the lottery. Isn't it obvious?
   c) The local beauty parlor and tannery does a pretty good job.
   d) Align with the universe.
   e) Get up at 5am every day. Run for two hours. Have one hard-boiled egg for breakfast. Think about what to do once you complete your Astrophysics PhD. Then head off to the beauty parlor.

7) When is it safe to stand in the middle of the Todd river in Alice Springs?
   a) Never. Don't even suggest people do that. Someone will end up killing themselves.
   b) Never. All the rivers in the Northern Territory of Australia are crocodile infested.
   c) Any day except Sunday. That's when the god-botherers are around.
   d) Most days – there's very rarely any water in the Todd River.

8) I said that a river without water is like a structure without...
   a) Cement.
   b) A MacDonald's nearby.
   c) Energy.
   d) Organization.
   e) A Trump logo.

9) I said that a dam on the river is ...
   a) Like a blocked drain.
   b) Like music to the ears of the renewable energy lobby.
   c) Upsetting to the environment.
   d) A metaphor for fear that will not allow you to put energy into moving forward.
   e) d and c.

10) I said that most humans' lives are, by default, run by ...
    a) The government
    b) The deep state shadow government
    c) Their kids and/or their parents
    d) Their unconscious dysfunctional beliefs, assumptions, concepts, and definitions
    e) Their fear about where their next meal is coming from
    f) Their mobile phone

11) I said that the innosense meditation takes you to...
    a) A place where members of whatever sex you're attracted to find you pretty cute.
    b) A place where you are beyond your dysfunctional mind and thoughts and feelings it creates and where it has no power.
    c) A Pleiadian light ship.
    d) Wherever you set the intention before you start.
    e) Rome. Because it's metaphysical law as well as physical law that all roads lead there.

12) I said that, for you humans, your shadows show up....
    a) Naturally around 5 o'clock.
    b) When the sun comes out.
    c) As part of a package deal with Cliff Richard.
    d) As a result of childhood wounding.

13) I said that the Sabotage Spotlight process is...
    a) A way to sabotage others.
    b) A way to see when others are sabotaging you.
    c) A way to start conflicts.
    d) A way to see the unconscious drivers of your dysfunctional behavior and self-sabotage.
    e) A way to see what drives other people's dysfunctional behavior.

14) Which of the following did I say is closest to the truth?
    a) Wishes only come true if you have a fairy godmother.
    b) All we can do is hope.
    c) If you fail to make a goal, you're a total failure and should be ashamed of yourself.
    d) According to Murphy's Law, 'Anything that can go wrong will go wrong' – so don't ever expect your plan to work out.
    e) A choice is a selection of one option over others; one possible future over every other possible future.
    f) None of the above.
    g) All of the above.

15) Creative tension is?
   a) When you dream of a painting you want to create but you just can't get out of bed.
   b) When you want to paint a painting and your partner wants you to paint the outside of the house.
   c) A band arguing about whose songs will make it onto the album.
   d) A fictitious reggae band that features in a future book I write with Vincent and he'd better start thinking about it and writing the songs now.
   e) The energetic difference between where you are now (current reality) and the end result of one of your choice(s).
   f) Definitely e and possibly d too.

16) A choice without energy is like …
   a) A fish without a bicycle.
   b) Nice puzzle, shame about the missing piece.
   c) The Todd River in Alice Springs – nice structure, shame about the water.
   d) None of the above.
   e) All of the above except c.

17) I said celebration is …
   a) My favorite 70's disco track.
   b) Only for real when the champagne is genuine French.
   c) A way to give your consciousness powerful positive messages.
   d) All you do in heaven.

18) You should 'do' your choices…
   a) Whenever you remember.
   b) Whenever it feels good and you feel in the flow.
   c) Every day unless you've got a really good excuse.
   d) Each day, every single day without fail.
   e) None of the above.

19) Sometimes, you will get action steps that don't seem to lead anywhere but will open you up to receive the ideas you need to move forwards
These might include ...
a) Gardening.
b) Exercising.
c) Journaling.
d) Taking a shower.
e) Working harder and really concentrating.
f) All the above except e.

20) When you see a big obstacle in front of you, (like a mountain when you're on the river) do you ...
a) Try and figure out how to blow it away.
b) Brace yourself to crash into it.
c) Find somewhere to stop and make a cunning plan.
d) Trust that the flow will carry you past the obstacle and that often you'll be guided to change direction in such a way that the obstacle is no longer in the way.

And, in case you are wondering how you went, the answers to the quiz are in
Appendix 3 Quiz answers

Epilogue

Over to you

Roxy

Have you wasted your money with this book?
Have you bought it, read it cover to cover and put it back down, deeply satisfied?
If that's all you do, then you've wasted your time and money.

That's not why Vincent and I were guided to write this.
Unlike much of my work, it wasn't created as an entertainment with a happy ending.

In fact, as you may have noticed, it doesn't really have an ending.
Why not?

Because it's over to you to create your own happy ending.
So take this book and the online exercises, do the work, engage with Vincent and his community for support, further training and coaching; and astonish yourself by creating your HeartVisio.

Good luck. With lots of love. Tough love.

And as you learn to get into the flow and hold yourself there, it will visit you in abundance.

Continuing your journey into intuition

Roxy

Colin Wilson, author of many books on the occult once defined magic as "the ability to live life guided by intuition."

This book gives you an entry point into connecting with your intuition and some of the foundational practices. There is so much more to learn and so many skills and techniques to practice.

Vincent and his collaborators will be running training and practice sessions, both in person and online that will help you continue your journey in living your life guided by intuition.

So please stay connected with Vincent by;

1) joining his community here https://www.facebook.com/groups/gettingintotheflowbook.

2) signing up for notifications and early bird discounts on upcoming events and trainings as well as Vincent's free insights, here
https://vincentgmelling.com/gitf-symbols-and-beyond

And finally, will there be a follow up book? You've read this book and seen all the work I want to cover with Vincent; and that he has a choice of creating a brand of books. So please watch the newsletter and join the Facebook group.

A final, super-synchronistic word from the Hopi elders

Vincent

    Here is another piece of magic. This came to me early in the revision process after the first published draft. It's a message, perfectly aligned to this book;

A prophecy given by Hopi Elders – June 8, 2000, Oraibi Arizona

You have been telling people that this is the Eleventh Hour, now you must go back and tell the people that this is the Hour. And there are things to be considered...

Where are you living?
What are you doing?
What are your relationships?
Are you in right relation?
Where is your water?

Know your garden.
It is time to speak your truth.
Create your community.
Be good to each other.
And do not look outside yourself for your leader.

Then he clasped his hands together, smiled, and said,
'This could be a good time!
There is a river flowing now very fast. It is so great and swift that there are those who will be afraid. They will try to hold on to the shore. They will feel they are being torn apart and will suffer greatly. Know the river has its destination. The elders say we must let go of the shore, push off into the middle of the river, keep our eyes open, and our heads above the water.

And I say, see who is in there with you and celebrate. At this time in history, we are to take nothing personally, least of all ourselves. For the moment that we do, our spiritual growth and journey come to a halt.

The time of the lone wolf is over. Gather yourselves! Banish the word "struggle" from your attitude and your vocabulary. All that we do now must be done in a sacred manner and in celebration.

We are the ones we've been waiting for.'

Appendices

Appendix 1

Exercises and resources

Facebook Group

Please join our Facebook group where you can share experiences and ask questions.

Thanks, Vincent and Roxy

https://www.facebook.com/groups/gettingintotheflowbook.

Innosense exercise

https://vincentgmelling.com/gitf-in-no-sense

All other exercises

This includes;

- Symbols
- Circles
- Spirit Guidance

https://vincentgmelling.com/gitf-symbols-and-beyond

Coaching Support

Here's the link for coaching enquiries;

https://vincentgmelling.com/vgm-coaching

Innosense meditation – guidelines and key steps

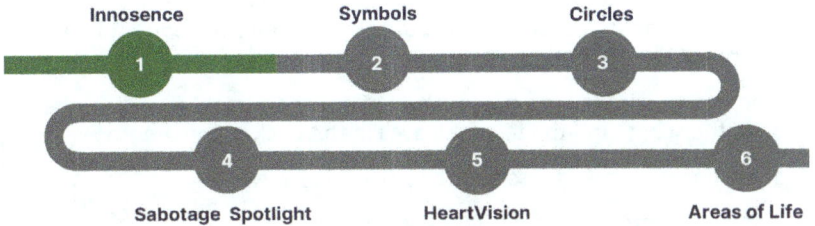

Innosense meditation – recap of key guidelines and key steps.

This meditation introduces you to the state of innosense in which your beliefs, assumptions and definitions are neutralized and you enter a powerful state where you are connected to intuition.

Guidelines

1. Be safe – don't do this driving, operating machinery or anything else
2. Be sober
3. Give yourself an hour to do this
4. If at all possible, do it in daylight
5. Ideally do it in nature
6. Be prepared to walk around and observe your surroundings
7. Be ready to journal your experience

Key steps

Have a notebook and pen handy

Come into a meditation position. If you're in a chair, have your legs and arms uncrossed. Lengthen your spine, soften the body, and take a couple of deep breaths.

Imagine you're walking in a forest. Just notice the sights, sounds, the feel, the scent, and the taste it leaves in the back of the mouth.

Imagine you come across a broad path. Follow it.

Imagine it comes to a fork. Take the left fork.

You come to the edge of the forest and in front of you is a meadow full of violet flowers. Start crossing the meadow.

Notice that the forest is far behind you and that some way in front of you there's a temple.

(continued)

You get to the temple. You ascend the steps that lead up to a very fine entrance. Enter the temple.

As you look around in the temple, you notice a crib. In the crib is a baby. As you look at the baby, you connect, heart to heart. Imagine yourself becoming one with the baby. And your mind becomes a child mind, innocent, clear, free from beliefs, assumptions, and other limitations.

Imagine now that the floor under you opens up and you begin to fall through a purple void, with the temple receding in the distance.

Keep imagining yourself falling, falling, falling.

Until you slow down and gently come back into your body.

Gently open your eyes, and head out into nature for twenty minutes. When you come back, journal the experience.

Practice coming out of innosense, diverting your attention; then going back into innosense three or four times. When you go back into innosense, you don't need to listen to the full meditation again. You just close your eyes, soften your body and set the intention that you are in innosense; and trust that you are.

Sabotage Spotlight Process

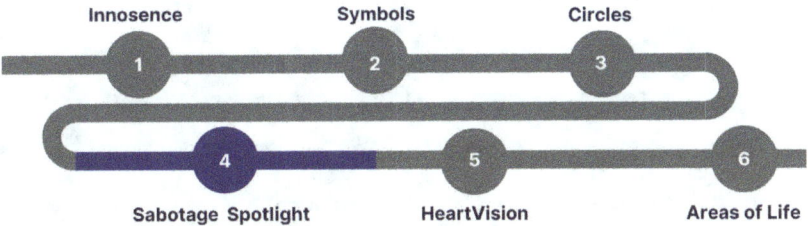

Key steps
This process shows up your unconscious processes — beliefs, assumptions, and definitions, and how they are shaping your reality.

Preparation steps
Identify a time when you didn't get what you wanted.
Get clear on what you did want at the time.

Process
1. List the thoughts – judgements, meanings that come up about you not getting what you wanted; and then the feelings and emotions that surface.
2. Identify what you make that mean about yourself, others involved in this and the world.
3. What's the underlying assumption I can't have <what I wanted> because <unconscious – limiting belief, assumption, definition, or combination>
4. Where's the power? The answer to this needs to reflect how you have sabotaged yourself by putting power in beliefs, assumptions, or definitions; after all, you didn't get what you wanted.
5. What's the end result? (that comes from where the power is)
6. From here, what would you love?
Maybe it's what you wanted in the first place. Maybe the situation has changed and you'd love something else.
7. Imaginatively create a circle of what you'd love to see exactly what it is. Then imaginatively rub that out and create a second circle, define it as the next step to get there and receive that intuitively

HeartVision meditation

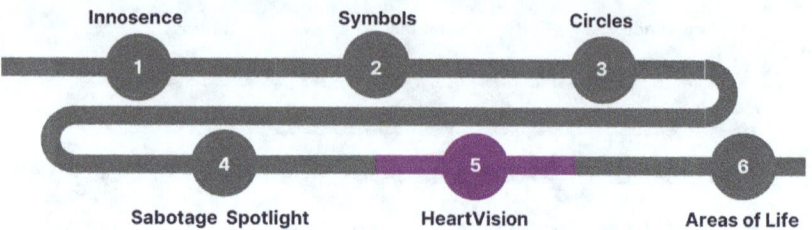

HeartVision meditation.

This meditation introduces you to your HeartVision, a vision of everything that you desire in your life and that it's true for you to choose.

Guidelines

1. Be safe — don't do this driving, operating machinery or anything else
2. Be sober
3. Give yourself an hour to do this
4. Be ready to journal your experience

Key steps

Have a notebook and pen handy.

Come into a meditation position. If you're in a chair, have your legs and arms uncrossed. Lengthen your spine, soften the body, and take a couple of deep breaths.

Imagine you're a blue mist. Take several seconds to feel into what it's like to be a blue mist, physically and emotionally. Imagine you're floating over a forest on a sunny day. Again, take a few moments to feel into this.

Now imagine that ahead of you, you see a mountain. As you drift closer, you see an entrance to a cave and you drift in to explore. The cave is large and well-lit and at the end is a tunnel leading down at an angle, into the depths of the mountain and you follow this tunnel down into the mountain. Down, down, and further down. Imagine yourself going even deeper into the mountain, down, down, further down.

Then the tunnel levels and start climbing at around forty-five degrees. As you follow the tunnel upwards, you begin to pick up speed. As you pick up speed your color turns to a paler blue. In the far distance, you see a pinprick of light — the end of the tunnel. You go faster and faster and as you go faster, you notice yourself becoming silvery bright. As you go faster still, you become transparent. The end of the tunnel appears larger, all of a sudden you find yourself coming out of the tunnel, slowing down and landing in your body.

You have journeyed to the land of the HeartVision where you will find everything that it true for you to have in life, everything that serves your true potential, and everything that serves you having and expressing your heart in the world.

Imagine you are greeted by a gatekeeper who gives you a gift. Take some time to explore the gift and the message it brings you.

And then step into the land of the HeartVision, pick up your pens and start journaling everything you find here.

Start writing, keep writing. Everything and everybody that is true for you to have in life is here. Keep the connection with your imagination open as you write what you see

Areas of Life meditation

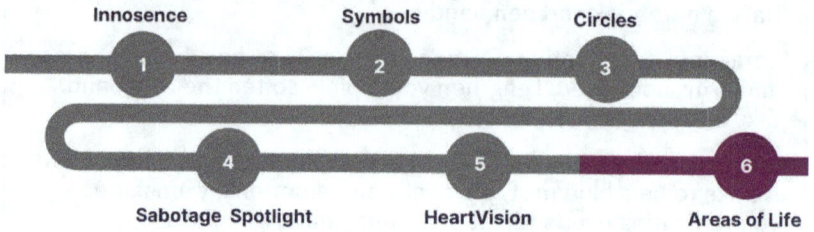

Areas of Life meditation.

This meditation takes you back into your HeartVision and what it shows up in specific areas of life. Pay attention to anything that jumps out at you or has a charge. You won't get that for every single suggestion but you should get something for each of the areas of life:-

- Relationships,
- Work and Career,
- Lifestyle,
- Recreation and Leisure,
- Artistic Expression and
- Personal qualities and beingness

Guidelines

1. Be safe — don't do this driving, operating machinery or anything else
2. Be sober
3. Give yourself an hour to do this
4. Be ready to journal your experience

Key steps

Have a notebook and pen handy.

Come into a meditation position. If you're in a chair, have your legs and arms uncrossed. Lengthen your spine, soften the body, and take a couple of deep breaths.

Come into innosense, a place where you're connected to everything through all time, space, and dimensions; and where the filters on everyday perception drop away and you're open to receive everything you need to know.

Now imagine a circle and define it as your HeartVision. Choose to be of service to your highest good and come from the heart and step in.

Imagine you're greeted by a gatekeeper, maybe the one you met in the HeartVision meditation, maybe not.

The gatekeeper guides you to a building and to the room in that building that's equipped as a home theater.

You sit down in a comfortable chair and the lights are dimmed until you're in the dark.

And the video presentation you're going to watch is called 'Areas of Life'. It's a summary and review of what was in your heart vision and what you may have missed on the way.

And so then you see a white title on a black screen that says 'Relationships'.

And after a few moments it fades to black.

You see a short video or a sequence of images that represent what you'd love for your intimate relationship, for relationships with your family, within communities you belong to and with friends.

Whatever you're shown is what you'd love from your heart whether you saw it before in the HeartVision meditation or, or whether you're being shown a fresh symbol.

Just notice what you're seeing, hearing and/or feeling, and notice whether it carries a charge for you — a sense that you have more to work on with this area of life. If you do, journal what you're getting.

When you're ready to move on, come back into the darkened home theater. Next see a white title on a black screen that says, "Work and Career".

And after a few moments it fades to black.

Take a few moments to reconnect with the state of innosense.

In your imagination, you see on the screen a short video or a sequence of images that represent what you'd love for your job, your career, work that gives you meaning and purpose and helps you express your true potential, work that takes what you do for fun, such as sport, travel or art and turns you into a professional.

Whatever you're shown is what you'd love from your heart whether you saw it before in the HeartVision meditation or, or whether you're being shown a fresh symbol.

Just notice what you're seeing, hearing and/or feeling, and notice whether it carries a charge for you — a sense that you have more to work on with this area of life. If you do, journal what you're getting.

When you're ready to move on, come back into the darkened home theater. Next see a white title on a black screen that says "Lifestyle".

And after a few moments it fades to black.

Take a few moments to reconnect with the state of innosense.

In your imagination, you see a short video or a sequence of images that represent what you'd love for your lifestyle, your home, your car, your possessions and how abundance shows up in your HeartVision.

Notice what you're seeing, hearing and/or feeling, and notice whether it carries a charge for you — a sense that you have more to work on with this area of life. If you do, journal what you're getting.

When you're ready to move on, come back into the darkened home theater. Next see a white title on a black screen that says, "Recreation and Leisure".

And after a few moments it fades to black.

Take a few moments to reconnect with the state of innosense.

In your imagination, you see a short video or a sequence of images that represent what you'd love for your recreation and leisure, sports, outdoor activities, travel, hobbies, whatever.

Whatever you're shown is what you'd love from your heart whether you saw it before in the HeartVision meditation or, or whether you're being shown a fresh symbol.

Notice what you're seeing, hearing and/or feeling, and notice whether it carries a charge for you — a sense that you have more to work on with this area of life. If you do, journal what you're getting.

When you're ready to move on, come back into the darkened home theater. Next see a white title on a black screen that says, "Artistic Expression".

And after a few moments it fades to black.

Take a few moments to reconnect with the state of innosense.

In your imagination, you see a short video or a sequence of images that represent any artistic expression that calls you — painting, drawing, performing arts, making music, writing, craftwork, whatever. Whatever you're shown is what you'd love from your heart whether you saw it before in the HeartVision meditation or, or whether you're being shown a fresh symbol.

Notice what you're seeing, hearing and/or feeling, and notice whether it carries a charge for you — a sense that you have more to work on with this area of life. If you do, journal what you're getting.

When you're ready to move on, come back into the darkened home theater. Next see a white title on a black screen that says, "Personal qualities and Beingness".

And after a few moments it fades to black.

Take a few moments to reconnect with the state of innosense.

In your imagination, you see a short video or a sequence of images that represent the personal qualities you'd love, how you are in the world, what the version of you in the end results of your choices looks like, what you'd love for health and self care. Whatever you're shown is what you'd love from your heart whether you saw it before in the HeartVision meditation or, or whether you're being shown a fresh symbol.

Notice what you're seeing, hearing and/or feeling, and notice whether it carries a charge for you — a sense that you have more to work on with this area of life. If you do, journal what you're getting.

So now this meditation is ended.

If you have some unpacking to do from the notes you made, you can do that now or come back another time, go into innosense and do it then.

And when that's all done you're ready to move on with the next steps – extracting your themes and creating your choices.

Spirit Guidance

This meditation takes you on an imaginative journey to meet a spirit guide and receive detailed guidance and wisdom from them which you will write down or record.

You don't have to believe in spirit guides; you can treat this as an imaginative exercise.

Guidelines

1. Have a notebook and pen handy, Dictation is also acceptable — do what works for you.
2. Ensure you have at least thirty minutes for the exercise.
3. Prepare a list of questions for your guides. You can ask them to get guidance on a choice, or get a flow of ideas for something you're creating. Add a general question such as 'What do I need to know to live in line with my purpose and true potential?'
4. The first part of the meditation up to entering the temple is the same as for the innosense meditation.

Key steps

Come into a meditation position. If you're in a chair, have your legs and arms uncrossed. Lengthen your spine, soften the body, and take a couple of deep breaths.

Imagine you're walking in a forest. Just notice the sights, sounds, the feel, the scent, and the taste it leaves in the back of the mouth.

Imagine you come across a broad path. Follow it.

Imagine it comes to a fork. Take the left fork.

You come to the edge of the forest and in front of you is a meadow full of violent flowers. Start crossing the meadow.

Notice that the forest is far behind you and that some way in front of you there's a temple.

(continued)

You get to the temple. You ascend the steps that lead up to a very fine entrance. Enter the temple.

Take in the temple. Notice the sights, sounds, the feel the scent of the temple and any taste that leaves in the back of the mouth.

Become aware of the presence of another being or beings with you.

Turn and greet them. Then find a place to settle and start asking the questions. Keep writing — the action of writing will open up your intuitive pipeline and the information you seek will flow through.

Appendix 2

Vincent's experience with the innosense meditation

Roxy

Please don't read this section until you've had a chance to do the innosense meditation out of doors in nature. This is intended as Vincent's personal share of his experiences, not as a how-to guide.

Vincent

The first time I did the innosense meditation was at a venue in North Sydney. It was very inner city; however, right outside the venue was a small square with a few large trees and flowers in pots and beds. When we had finished the meditation, this is what first met our eyes and I was amazed. I'd never experienced such vibrancy in nature before — the colors were intense and there was a powerful energetic feel about the plants and trees. The leaves felt they were straining to sunbathe in the maximum possible amount of sunlight.

I remember seeing and feeling the bark on the trees in all its complexity and the fine detail in the leaves — the veins and coloration — in a way that I had never seen them before; or at least not since childhood. I noticed insects crawling across them and was entranced by their apparent sense of purpose.

Another time that I did this exercise was in Eswatini (formerly Swaziland) in southern Africa. I remember the entrancing and flourishing floral gardens, and, in particular, spending what seemed like hours mesmerized by a bougainvillea which drew me in. I remember the fascination with the petals, and the way that the coloration changed from the upper part of the petal down towards the base in a way that I'd never really noticed before.

It's not just natural objects that I saw more profoundly. In North Sydney, I recall taking in a motorcycle in that way for the very first time. It was obviously somebody's pride and joy, sparkling clean with gleaming chrome. I spent an age contemplating all the little parts and how they all fitted together and how little pipes came out here and went to there. Then I was captivated by the controls and how elegantly they seem to be laid out. Especially as I've never really taken an interest in motorcycles.

There were a host of mechanical parts that I would struggle to understand from mental place but in an innosense, I began to wonder at beauty of it all, at how it must all connect together to create this wonderful powerful machine.

I'd love to know how you went with the meditation. Please leave a share in the Facebook group.

Appendix 3

Quiz answers

Roxy

Seriously? You need the answers to the quiz?

Were you reading the book?

Aren't the right answers obvious?

Well then, aren't the wrong answers obvious?

Do you seriously expect me to believe that you believe that I said that the way you create the greatest most beautiful version of yourself is to drink a couple of bottles of vodka, look in the mirror and tell yourself how amazing you look?

However, at the insistence of Vincent's publisher, here you are:

1. Why would you want to get into the flow?
   Answer — c) Because the universe will help you with synchronicities, coincidences, and opportunities.

2. Why does the universe help you when you're in the flow?
   Answer c) – Because it's creative, expanding and evolving and you're aligning with those forces.
   The book says nothing about unicorns; but do check them out on YouTube.

3. What did I say was wrong with sitting on the couch and visualizing millions of dollars coming to you?
   Answer e) Nothing. I'm not judgmental. Although it is a total waste of time.

4. How did I say the universe started out?
   Answer e) It started out with the Big Bang.

5. How much money did I say it cost to create the universe?
    Answer c) The universe didn't need money to create itself.

6. How do you create the greatest most beautiful version of yourself?
    Answer d) Align with the universe.

7. When is it safe to stand in the middle of the Todd River in Alice Springs?
    Answer d) Most days — there's very rarely any water in the Todd River.

8. I said that a river without water is like a structure without...
    Answer — c) Energy.

9. I said that a dam on the river is ...
    Answer e) – d and c. which were
    Upsetting to the environment.
    Fear that will not allow you to put energy into moving forward.

10. I said that most humans' lives are, by default, run by ...
    Answer c) Their dysfunctional beliefs, assumptions, concepts, and definitions

11. I said that the innosense meditation takes you to...
    Answer b) A place where you are beyond your dysfunctional mind and thoughts and feelings it creates and where it has no power.

12. I said that, for you humans, your shadows show up....
    Answer d) As a result of childhood wounding.

13. I said that the Sabotage Spotlight process is...
    Answer d) A way to see the unconscious drivers of your dysfunctional behavior and self-sabotage.

14. Which of the following is closest to the truth?
    Answer d) A choice is a selection of one option over others; one possible future over every other possible future.

15. Creative tension is?
    Answer e) The energetic difference between where you

are now (current reality) and the end result of one of your choice(s).
I am serious when I said Vincent would be writing about a fictitious reggae band too — but it wasn't in the book

16. A choice without energy is like ...
    Answer c) The Todd River in Alice Springs — nice structure, shame about the water.

17. I said celebration is ...
    Answer c) A way to give your consciousness powerful positive messages.

18. You should 'do' your choices...
    Answer d) Each day, every single day without fail.

19. Sometimes, you will get action steps that don't seem to lead anywhere but will open you up to receive the ideas you need to move forwards.
    These might include...
    Answer f) All the above except e — so any of. Gardening, exercising, journaling, taking a shower.

20. When you see a big obstacle in front of you, (like a mountain when you're on the river) do you ...
    Answer d) Trust that the flow will carry you past the obstacle and that often you'll be guided to change direction and the obstacle is no longer in the way.

Riveting, wasn't it?

How did you score?

20	You're a powerful cosmic multidimensional mega-being or an ascended master
5-19	You're only a human. Humans!
0-4	Try rereading the book

About the author(s)

Vincent by Vincent

Vincent was born into a world that put a high value on working hard. As a cub scout, he remembers shouting, "we will do our best" at the start of each meeting. Although the society he was brought up in equated working hard with doing your best, Vincent was never fully convinced.

Throughout his career in IT and Project Management, he observed repeatedly that the outcome of working hard and doing your best was usually stress, burnout and being taken for granted. Others seemed to have some sort of magical gift that put them in the right place at the right time without having to work especially hard and not being any smarter. But the dirty secret was, they all ended up with more money, to be sure, more stress, greater burnout and fully overwhelmed.

Vincent started his intuitive journey in 2013 with William Whitecloud and completed coaching-level training in 2015. He has increased his mastery of the work since then, teaching and coaching and is also accredited with the International Coaching Federation.

This was the perfect preparation for the journey into the flow that the universe dumped on him as described in Part 1. What has astonished him even more is that the flow did not stop when he disembarked at Melbourne's Tullamarine airport at the end of the trip. First there was the intuitive demand to write this book; and then the magic continued to flow throughout the writing, revision, and publishing journey.

It is this magic that Vincent has come to believe is how humanity should harness and live by but has forgotten; and he sees his purpose as reminding them of it.

In his spare time — what spare time? Despite his belief that success doesn't come just from working hard, Vincent loves writing so much he never has any spare time and a backlog of follow-on books Roxy wants him to create.

Vincent lives in, and loves Melbourne, Australia.

Roxy by Vincent

Roxy the muse has been working with humans pretty much as long as humans have been around, one of the first muses to arrive to work on the planet.

As a super-powerful light being, she has always seen her role as bringing humans to an awareness of their own greatness, inner power, and divinity and also to an awareness of their frailties, and the stories they tell themselves as they sabotage their lives.

Wordsworth's well known poem 'Daffodils' is a wonderful example of the arresting quality of nature and how humans resonate and respond from their greatness. On the other hand, Shakespeare's plays, particularly the tragedies with their flawed protagonists, illustrate how profoundly humans are controlled by their shadow, and the stories they make up about themselves.

Roxy has worked with Persian magi, the sophists of ancient Greece, John of Patmos, author of the biblical Book of Revelation, and St Augustine of Hippo before leaving the world of religion and philosophy to help steer emerging renaissance literature. She helped Michel de Montaigne developed the essay form in the mid-1580s as well as Shakespeare. She went on to help Isaac Newton with his alchemical manuscripts before helping the romantic movement of the late 18th and early 19th centuries. In the modern era, she has worked with Carl Jung and Robert M Pirsig amongst others.

These are the well-known authors of the western world; but Roxy has worked all over the planet through the ages with much of her work never seeing the light of day.

As literacy has risen, especially since the invention of the printing press, and again with the advent of the internet, Roxy has helped induct many new muses who have come to help working with humans. Through this network, she has established a boutique clientele of writers who have works that cry out for her particular skills and expertise.

Roxy has come to this book because she understands that time has come for humans to start living in their true power and greatness and, unless they do, humanity as a species is doomed.

What Roxy loves most — holding humans in the energy of their greatness.

What Roxy most dislikes — having to work so diligently to hold humans in the energy of their greatness, as they fight so hard to sabotage themselves — and call that freedom.

Roxy by Roxy

Oh. So I'm just Vincent's imaginary friend am I?

Vincent wasn't going to include me in the author's bios?

Is it not clear to you that I wrote most of this book.

I infused it with wisdom, humor, class, and star power.

I suppose you want to know who I am and what my story is.

Am I a spirit guide? Yes. Although some of you may think I'm just a crazed creation of Vincent's over-fertile imagination.

You make your own mind up. It's no skin off my nose, not that I have skin in the literal sense, or a nose, that's just what you humans say.

Let's just say this isn't my first book — I've worked with many authors over the years.

Do you want to know a long-time secret?
Solve a long-time riddle?
Settle a long time controversy?
Well it was me and a couple of fellow muses that wrote all the Shakespearian work.
Seriously. You must know, everybody knows it wasn't really him.

He'd say I wrote with him but I did all the heavy lifting.

Did you know Henry V starts out;

> *"O, for a muse of fire that would ascend*
> *The brightest heaven of invention"*.

That was my cue. He got me to work with him. I did some powerful work on Henry V didn't I?

Who else have I worked with?

I'm a muse, It's work. That's what we do.

I've worked with many, many, many famous and not so famous writers. If you read this book, you'd know about some of them. Even now, when I'm not working with Vincent, I'm working with a dozen other humans across the planet and in multiple languages.

How old am I?

Have I lived on earth?

Have I been an alien?

Keep sending in the questions. I haven't told Vincent yet but I have him down to help me with my autobiography.

Vincent by Roxy

Now on the other hand, if you want to know a bit about Vincent

Let me say that I'm torn between telling you about his amazing empathic qualities, his academic achievement, his professionalism, his high intelligence both regular and intuitive, his creative ability... ...and the honest truth.

Let me just say that I've enjoyed working with him. In a way. He knows his place. He's moderately good at typing up what I give him. With a little, no a lot of prodding he can be a good – no, acceptable – worker too. Now I could work twenty-four hours a day seven days a week but he's only a human, and as I often have to remind him, I do have an eternity, whereas he doesn't. And I'll admit I may appear to be a bit overpowering at times.

Now you probably want to know where he was born (Brighton UK), what school he went to (cannot be named for legal reasons especially as he was slapped on the back of his legs on his very first day so has been in trouble with his educators from the very start), what his English teachers thought about him (he'd never amount to much), all his accomplishments (a mercifully short list), his personal life (as I've said this is a serious metaphysical text, not a dating profile) and all those other details that are sure to turn up in his Wikipedia entry. I promise you he will have one.

Vincent's ambitions are pretty much irrelevant. He's an author now and has work to do with me. It's all in his highest good.

In his spare time, Vincent likes to... Spare time? His limiting beliefs do not allow him spare time. Although he somehow manages to create space for his spiritual practice, shaking aka bio-energy meditation, and kundalini yoga in which he's a certified teacher. And he manages to make time to connect with his children, grandchildren, and extended family.

Acknowledgements

This book would not have been written without the generous support and encouragements of a legion of friends, family and connections. Thanks to you all.

I would particularly like to extend my thanks to those of you that have contributed directly to this book in special ways :-

First, I would like to thank Pat Grayson of Heartspace Publications. You gave me the confidence to take this from first draft to published book and beyond; and the advice and feedback I needed to bring it into its final form. And to Ruanna Segal for recommending me to you and connecting us up. A true piece of magic.

I would especially like to thank from my heart the members of the writing group I've worked with past and present – Leah Foley, Cher Chin; Jamie Louise Willis, Stev Fioretti, Kath Hall, and Phillipa Tate-Gilder. Your support and contributions were an essential part of the structure I needed to keep the book moving forward, onward and upward. You guys rock and I wish you all the best for your own books.

I would also like to thank Keely McKinnon from Green Hill publications for her work on the cover; and Maria Simms of Laurel Cohn and Ian Mathieson for their editing work and suggestions.

I would also like to thank Roxy for her contribution and all her valuable insights.

Next, I would like to thank all those whose influence has created the foundation on which it has been built.

I would like to acknowledge and thanks to William Whitecloud, creator of Natural Success, a life-changing intuition-based training modality that opened me up to receiving this book; and, also, for his training 'Meet Your Writer's Genius', which was an immense help and inspiration in putting it together. Thanks, William for all the teachings, the profound lessons and adventures over the years.

I would like to thank all the members of the Natural Success community that you created and that I've connected with, worked with and who have been so supportive over the years. My special thanks go to Ian and Bahar McIntyre for their support and encouragement as I first stepped into facilitating this work.

I would also especially like to thank from my heart my co-collaborators, past and present, in the Academy of Intuitive Mastery – Leah Foley, Tess Miller-Sharp, Jonathan Miller and Lou Iacono. I have learned so much from you and grown so much and can't wait to work with you on our advanced trainings.

I would also like to acknowledge and thank Robert Fritz whose book *The Path of Least Resistance* has been an inspiration and source of deep understanding of the mechanics of creating.

Thanks to all you wonderful people I met on the Melbourne Standup Comedy circuit in 2013-4 especially Robbie Gualtieri and Brad Oakes for the weekly workshops they used to run. I've been able to integrate many skills and lessons learned in that time and that has been foundational to the writing of this book.

I would also like to acknowledge Angela, an English teacher from my early teens for her encouragement in the development of my writing skills at that formative age.

Lastly, I would like to thank all those who have influenced me in a positive way in my journey.

Thanks to all my shaking family who have supported me in the practice over the years and to Ratu Bagus who created it and has since passed. Shaking has kept me sane, energized and led me to the home where I wrote this book.

Sharon Goyen has supported and encouraged me in so many ways over the years – thank you.

I would love to express my deepest gratitude for my paternal grandmother and her siblings and their families. They were renowned for their sense of humor and that has surfaced through me in this book. And, finally, thanks to my siblings, my children and partners, and my nephews and nieces for their love, support and for staying out of the way until it was too late to stop me publishing this book.

Glossary

Chaos Magick	Chaos magick is an approach to magick that was formulated in the late 1970's in the UK. It is grounded in the writings and beliefs of artist Austin Osman Spare in the early-mid-1900s. The founders considered that existing traditions of magick had become overly arcane and embellished and they sought to peel away all those layers to leave a simplified, easy-to-use set of beliefs, processes and techniques.
Chi	Chi (also spelled Qi) is the name for life force energy in Traditional Chinese Medicine and also in martial arts. It is considered to flow through meridians or channels in the body; and, if the flow is interrupted, this manifests as various forms of ill-health.
Creative Tension	A creative structure in consciousness has a starting point or current reality and an end result. With all creative structures there is a force in consciousness that pulls reality from the starting point towards the end result. This force is creative tension and it always tries to resolve in favor of the end result.
HeartVision	A vision that comes from the inner spirit or genius (as opposed to a vision born out the parts of us in lack or neediness). Also known as a Land of Plenty.
Innosense	Innosense is spelled this way as a concatenation of 'in no sense'. This is because the innosense meditation tales us out of the place where our limiting beliefs, assumptions and definitions could cause us to judge the information we get and into a non-judgemental state where we're opened up to receive information from our intuition.

Kundalini energy	Kundalini means coiled snake. In yogic philosophy, it is a form of divine feminine energy located at the base of the spine. Normally is it dormant and can be awakened by various yogic practices. In most of these, the kundalini is awakened gently and is felt as heat and physical energy, often combined with laughter. While many seek a full kundalini awakening and it can be a transformational experience, it does carry the risk of physical side-effects (kundalini syndrome) that are not well understood by doctors. [1]
Magi	The plural form of magus. A magus was a Zoroastrian priest from ancient Persia (Iran). These priests were known for their interest in esoteric and arcane wisdom, astrology, and magic Magi, is used in Christianity as another name for the three wise men, or kings, who visited the baby Jesus in Bethlehem. Christians celebrate this as the feast of the Epiphany.
Mana	A Hawaiian word meaning spiritual energy or life force.
Ojas	Ojas means 'essence of vitality' and is a particularly subtle form of energy in the body. It gives us our immunity, strength, and happiness.
Prana	Prana means vital life force energy. Yogic practice encourages the accumulation of prana for health and vitality. The most common practice for this is pranayama (literally control of the breath) which covers a variety of breathwork practices taught in yoga classes. Prana can come from other sources, for example in our food. It flows through energy channels in the body called nadis. (similar to chi in Chinese medicine).

---

[1] This blog article has good information about kundalini syndrome
https://saiayurvedic.com/blog/kundalini-syndrome-the-dangers-of-unpreparedness.aspx

Reiki	Reiki means universal life force energy. It is an energy healing modality in which the practitioner channels chi energy through the client, using a series of hand positions, to promote physical and mental health.
Sabotage Spotlight	A tool that helps the user identify which limiting beliefs, definitions, assumptions, and other mental constructs block progress. Also known as the Conflict Deconstruction process.
Sex energy	In traditions ranging from Tantra to magick, there is powerful subtle energy that comes from sexual arousal that can be transmuted or harnessed to help us in other areas of life through intention.
Tantric lovemaking	A ritual form of lovemaking that incorporates meditation and eyegazing, and the energy of which can be transmuted or harnessed to manifest intentions. It is noted for being prolonged (sometimes hours long) by avoiding explosive orgasms (male ejaculation, clitoral orgasms) that are over quickly and leave participants feeling sleepy and depleted in favor of implosive orgasms where the energy is held up in the body and can create ecstatic experiences.

Work further with Vincent

Workshops and Training

Vincent offers various intuition workshops and trainings through the year both on his own and as a founding member of the Academy of Intuitive Mastery. These include trainings in basic intuition skills, creating and working with your HeartVision, supercharging your creative momentum and also Masterclasses. Future trainings are planned to cover leadership and coaching accreditation and creating a transformational business.

On his own, Vincent also offers a range of masterclasses You can find an up-to-date list of what's coming up here :-

https://vincentgmelling.com/vgm-calendar

Coaching and consultations

Coaching gives clients the benefits of creating their true vision, accountability for their progress, reflection to identify where they sabotage themselves and the opportunity to learn advanced tools on an as needs basis.

There are more details and an enquiry form at this link …

https://vincentgmelling.com/vgm-coaching

Reach out to Vincent

Speaking engagements

Vincent is available for speaking engagements both on topics related to the content of this book and any other topics of mutual interest. You can reach him here :-

https://vincentgmelling.com/speaking-engagements

Media Enquiries

If you're in the media – national, local, online or social – Vincent would love to help you out with interviews, blog posts or other contributions. Vincent's happy to contribute to TV, radio, magazines, podcasts, social media, summits, conferences, guest blogs and whatever's coming next that hasn't even been thought of yet. You can reach him here :-

https://vincentgmelling.com/media-enquiries

www.ingramcontent.com/pod-product-compliance
Lightning Source LLC
Chambersburg PA
CBHW071954290426
44109CB00018B/2014